nickelodeon

ARE YOU SMARTER THAN A 5TH GRADER

THE

ULTIMATE COMPANION

QUIZ BOOK

TABLE OF CONTENTS

ARE YOU SMARTER THAN A 5TH GRADER

Welcome to *Are You Smarter Than a 5th Grader*! The show that gives grown-ups the chance to win $100,000 by testing their smarts and proving that they are smarter than a 5th grader.

To play, each contestant faces different subjects, starting with the 1st-Grade level and going all the way to the 5th-Grade level. Before each grade level begins, the contestant chooses one of their classmates to help.

The questions are taken straight from grade-school textbooks, randomly mixed among open-ended, multiple-choice, and true/false questions.

> 1st–2nd Grade: 1 question each
> 3rd–4th Grade: 2 questions each

> In 1st–4th Grade, the contestant receives 2 cheats: COPY and PEEK.

- If a contestant chooses to COPY, they use their classmate's answer, sight unseen.

- If a contestant chooses to PEEK, they are shown their classmate's answer and can choose to use that answer or not.

- If the contestant gets a question right, they earn the money at stake and move up the ladder. But if they get a question wrong, they stay at their current level, and continue on with their questions!

After all 1st- through 4th-Grade questions are asked, it's time for the 5th-Grade questions . . . and the chance to multiply the money a contestant has already won!

5th Grade: 5 questions to answer with 60 seconds on the clock. The right answers won't be revealed until all 5 answers are locked in!

- The money is multiplied 2×, 3×, 4×, 5×, 10× with each correct answer.

- If a contestant isn't confident with their answer, they have one cheat available to them. This is played just like a PEEK, where the contestant can go with their classmate's answer or choose one of their own, at which point we'll see if they are correct or not.

Now it's your turn to test your smarts! Turn the page and find out if you're smarter than a 5th grader!

$10,000

$5,000

$2,500

$1,000

$500

$250

MEET THE CLASSMATES

SAYA

FAVORITE SUBJECTS
- Vocabulary
- History

SKILLS / FACTS
- Contortionist
- Detailed character artist
- Speaks fluent Japanese

PATRICK

FAVORITE SUBJECTS
- Vocabulary
- Grammar

SKILLS / FACTS
- Fascinated by dinosaurs
- Plays the trumpet
- Kung Fu master

COLIN

FAVORITE SUBJECTS
- Social Studies
- Anatomy

SKILLS / FACTS
- Boxer
- Pinewood Derby car champ
- Champion swimmer

MIA

FAVORITE SUBJECTS
- Science
- English

SKILLS / FACTS
- Published poet
- Plays the harp
- Runs cross-country

TRISTAN

FAVORITE SUBJECTS
- History
- Math

SKILLS / FACTS
- Tae Kwon Do master
- Has pet bearded dragons
- Created a rap song about the show

COOPER

FAVORITE SUBJECTS
- Math
- Health

SKILLS / FACTS
- President of his class
- Juggler
- Push-up pro

AMIRA

FAVORITE SUBJECTS
- Reading
- Science

SKILLS / FACTS
- Wants to find life outside of Earth
- Wants to work for NASA
- Honor roll student

QUINNE

FAVORITE SUBJECTS
- Vocabulary
- Reading

SKILLS / FACTS
- Wants to be a roller coaster engineer
- Built a skate ramp in her yard
- Drummer in a band

JAMIR

FAVORITE SUBJECTS
- Grammar
- Science

SKILLS / FACTS
- Aspiring action star
- Has a funny nickname
- Bow tie fanatic

CHLOE

FAVORITE SUBJECTS
- Literature
- Math

SKILLS / FACTS
- Does stand-up comedy
- MMA champ
- Speaks Mandarin

NICK

FAVORITE SUBJECTS
- History
- Geography

SKILLS / FACTS
- Loves game shows
- Kayaker
- Hip-Hop dancer

ISABELLA

FAVORITE SUBJECTS
- Reading
- History

SKILLS / FACTS
- Salsa dancer
- Has won multiple pageants
- Loves sloths

AMAZING ANIMALS!

A IS FOR ANIMALS

1   Natural fleece comes from the hair grown by which of the following animals?

    a. sheep

    b. caterpillars

    c. silkworms

2   Which of the following animals is a quadruped?

    a. elephant

    b. flamingo

    c. honeybee

3   A fawn is the specific name for the young of which of the following animals?

    a. deer

    b. duck

    c. swan

4   Genetically, which of the following animals is most closely related to humans?

    a. apes

    b. dolphins

    c. dogs

5   Which of the following animals does not produce wool?

    a. goat

    b. sheep

    c. cow

6   An iguana is a member of which of the following classes of animal?

    a. reptile

    b. amphibian

    c. fish

7 The rhinoceros is native to two continents. Asia is one of those continents. Which of the following is the other?

    a. Africa

    b. South America

    c. Australia

8 Which of the following animals is a rodent?

    a. badger

    b. groundhog

    c. marmoset

9 Ocelots belong to what animal family?

    a. cat

    b. lizard

    c. marsupial

10 Which of the following animals is a primate?

    a. baboon

    b. squirrel

    c. salmon

11 Which of the following is the term for a baby koala?

    a. johnny

    b. jimmy

    c. joey

12 A nautilus is an example of which of the following?

    a. insect

    b. mollusk

    c. reptile

13 Which of the following is the closest living relative to the trilobite?

    a. African elephant

    b. gecko

    c. horseshoe crab

14 What land mammal has the largest ears?

15 The emu is native to what continent also known for its marsupials?

16 What massive relative of the deer known for its antlers is the state animal of Maine?

17 The salamander is not a reptile, but belongs to what class of animal?

18 By definition, a buck, a doe, and a joey comprise a family of what animal?

19 What material are spiderwebs made of?

20 What species of bear is pictured here?

25 In terms of average weight, what is the largest living land animal native to North America?

26 Lemurs are native to two island nations off the coast of what continent?

27 The epidermis is the outer layer of skin on mammals. What is the word for the layer immediately beneath the epidermis?

21 What land mammal has, on average, the longest neck?

22 What species of animal is the only striped wild cat?

23 If Mia snaps a photo of a laughing hyena in its native habitat, she is visiting what continent?

24 Wombats are native to what continent?

28 In Anna Sewell's novel *Black Beauty*, the title character is what species of animal?

29 If a cod, a shrimp, and a seal make up a typical food chain, which animal is in the middle of the chain?

BONUS
THE WORD "REYNARD" REFERS TO WHAT SPECIES OF ANIMAL?

30 TRUE OR FALSE? Caterpillars are insects.

31 TRUE OR FALSE? Cows can sleep standing up.

32 TRUE OR FALSE? Manatees are mammals.

33 TRUE OR FALSE? Owls typically hunt at night.

34 TRUE OR FALSE? Bats have feathers on their wings.

35 TRUE OR FALSE? Polar bears are native to both the north and south poles.

36 TRUE OR FALSE? Dolphins, which are marine mammals, typically have teeth.

37 TRUE OR FALSE? Male cows produce milk.

38 TRUE OR FALSE? A porpoise is a species of fish.

39 TRUE OR FALSE? The hippopotamus is a reptile.

40 TRUE OR FALSE? Some frogs hibernate.

41 TRUE OR FALSE? A butterfly is not an insect.

42 TRUE OR FALSE? A wild boar is a species of pig.

43 TRUE OR FALSE? Chimpanzees are members of the ape family.

44 **TRUE OR FALSE?** A female frog lays its eggs in the water.

45 **TRUE OR FALSE?** A mallard is a species of duck.

46 **TRUE OR FALSE?** Bats nurse their babies with milk.

47 **TRUE OR FALSE?** Male howler monkeys can howl louder than female howler monkeys.

48 **TRUE OR FALSE?** Lions are native only to Africa.

49 **TRUE OR FALSE?** A female fox is called a vixen.

50 **TRUE OR FALSE?** Some dolphins live in rivers.

51 **TRUE OR FALSE?** A falcon is a species of hawk.

52 **TRUE OR FALSE?** By definition, an "owlet" is a term that refers to a young owl.

53 **TRUE OR FALSE?** Giraffes have the same number of vertebrae in their necks as humans.

54 **TRUE OR FALSE?** Clams have backbones.

EVERYTHING
REPTILES

1. **TRUE OR FALSE?** TURTLES HAVE BACKBONES.

2. **TRUE OR FALSE?** ALLIGATORS USE BOTH GILLS AND LUNGS TO BREATHE.

3. **TRUE OR FALSE?** CROCODILES HATCH FROM EGGS.

4. IN TERMS OF SIZE AND WEIGHT, LEATHERBACKS ARE THE LARGEST SPECIES OF WHAT REPTILE?

5 **TRUE OR FALSE?** SNAKES SMELL WITH THEIR TONGUES.

6 **TRUE OR FALSE?** A CROCODILE AND AN ALLIGATOR ARE MEMBERS OF THE SAME SPECIES.

7 **TRUE OR FALSE?** SOME SNAKES HIBERNATE FOR THE WINTER.

8 IN TERMS OF AVERAGE SIZE, WHAT SPECIES IS THE LARGEST LIVING MEMBER OF THE LIZARD FAMILY?

9 SNAKES ARE COLD-BLOODED ANIMALS. WHICH OF THESE IS ANOTHER WORD FOR "COLD-BLOODED"?

A. ECTOTHERMIC   B. HYPOTHERMIC   C. ENDOTHERMIC

10 WHAT VENOMOUS LIZARD IS NAMED FOR A RIVER BASIN THAT EXTENDS FROM NEW MEXICO TO ARIZONA?

DEEP IN THE OCEAN

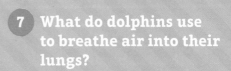

1. **TRUE OR FALSE?** If you had a pet humpback whale, your pet would be a type of fish.

2. In which of these sea creatures would a pearl occur naturally?

   a. crab

   b. oyster

   c. starfish

3. **TRUE OR FALSE?** Sea otters have gills.

4. In terms of length and weight, which of the following is the largest marine animal?

   a. giant squid

   b. great white shark

   c. blue whale

5. **TRUE OR FALSE?** Fish are cold-blooded animals.

6. **TRUE OR FALSE?** Aside from their teeth, sharks do not have any bones in their bodies.

7. What do dolphins use to breathe air into their lungs?

   a. gills

   b. snout

   c. blowhole

8. **TRUE OR FALSE?** Fish use gills to breathe in water.

9. **TRUE OR FALSE?** Lobsters are vegetarians.

10. A crayfish is a species of which of the following?

    a. crustacean

    b. fish

    c. mollusk

11 Hammerhead and thresher are both species of what predatory fish?

12 **TRUE OR FALSE?** The marine animal known as coral is an invertebrate.

13 **TRUE OR FALSE?** If SpongeBob SquarePants were a real sea sponge, he'd have no brain.

14 What species of animal is the largest member of the dolphin family?

15 Which of the following is considered a cetacean?

    a. blue whale

    b. great white shark

    c. shrimp

16 Natural pearls are formed inside which of the following animals?

    a. arthropods

    b. crustaceans

    c. mollusks

17 An adult boto dolphin is typically what unique color?

    a. black

    b. green

    c. pink

18 A phylum is a group of similar animal classes. Starfish and sea urchins belong to what phylum of animals whose name derives from the Greek for "spiny" and "skin"?

19 The octopus belongs to what class of animals?

BONUS
WHAT IS THE LOUDEST ANIMAL IN THE WORLD?

BIRD WATCHING

1   HOW MANY WINGS DOES A TOUCAN HAVE?

2   **TRUE OR FALSE?** THE HUMMINGBIRD LAYS THE SMALLEST EGGS OF ANY BIRD.

3   IF COLIN AND AMIRA EACH HAVE A PAIR OF PET PARAKEETS, AND THEIR FRIEND QUINNE HAS A PARTRIDGE, HOW MANY BIRDS DO THE THREE HAVE IN TOTAL?

4   A GANDER IS THE MALE OF WHAT SPECIES OF BIRD?

5   HOW MANY PAIRS OF WINGS DOES A HUMMINGBIRD HAVE?

6   **TRUE OR FALSE?** PENGUINS ARE BIRDS.

7   **TRUE OR FALSE?** ALL SPECIES OF BIRDS LAY EGGS.

8   IN TERMS OF HEIGHT, WHAT IS THE WORLD'S LARGEST SPECIES OF LIVING BIRD?

9   **TRUE OR FALSE?** ALL BIRDS BUILD NESTS.

10 THE TREE-DWELLING ANIMAL KNOWN AS A SLOTH IS WHICH OF THE FOLLOWING?

      A. REPTILE   B. BIRD   C. MAMMAL

11 AN EGRET IS WHICH OF THE FOLLOWING TYPES OF ANIMAL?

      A. BIRD   B. MAMMAL   C. REPTILE

12 CLUTCHING A SNAKE IN ITS MOUTH, WHAT BIRD IS FEATURED ON THE NATIONAL FLAG OF MEXICO?

ALL ABOUT BUGS

1 TRUE OR FALSE? Insects are members of the animal kingdom.

2 The name of which of the following insects is also a compound word?
a. mosquito
b. hornet
c. butterfly

3 The majority of ants in an ant colony are of what gender?

4 Monarch, swallowtail, and painted lady are all variations of what kind of insect?

BONUS THERE ARE FOUR STAGES IN A BUTTERFLY'S LIFE CYCLE. WHAT IS THE STAGE IMMEDIATELY AFTER CATERPILLAR?

5 TRUE OR FALSE? When a queen ant lays her eggs, worker ants in the colony will typically help keep them clean and warm.

6 A typical ant has how many legs?

7 Which of the following is not an insect?
a. moth
b. millipede
c. dragonfly

8 TRUE OR FALSE? Some insects have hearts.

9 Tristan has 15 earthworms. Chloe has 20 more earthworms than Tristan. What is the total number of earthworms they have combined?
a. 35
b. 50
c. 65

10 TRUE OR FALSE? Honeybees that leave the hive to collect pollen are male.

11 TRUE OR FALSE? The larva of a fly is called a maggot.

12 TRUE OR FALSE? In the life cycle of a typical butterfly, the adult stage immediately follows the caterpillar stage.

13 There are three main body parts of an insect. The thorax and abdomen are two. What is the third?

14 TRUE OR FALSE? Drone bees are male.

15 With more than 300,000 different types of species, which is the largest order of insects in the world?
a. moth
b. fly
c. beetle

16 If an ant colony's population doubles every 3 days, and it has 40,000 ants on day 15, how many ants did it have on day 9?

CATS & DOGS

1 TRUE OR FALSE? THE DOMESTIC CAT AND THE CATFISH ARE MEMBERS OF THE SAME CLASS OF ANIMALS.

2 A CAT IS TO A KITTEN AS A GOAT IS TO WHICH OF THE FOLLOWING?

A. CUB   B. CALF   C. KID

3 IF PATRICK'S DOG, PETE, IS 14 DOG YEARS OLD, AND 1 HUMAN YEAR EQUALS 7 DOG YEARS, HOW MANY HUMAN YEARS OLD IS PETE?

4 TRUE OR FALSE? A GUINEA PIG IS A TYPE OF PIG.

5 PERSIAN, SIAMESE, AND ABYSSINIAN ARE ALL BREEDS OF WHAT ANIMAL?

6 IF 6 DOGS EACH BURIED 4 BONES, WHAT IS THE TOTAL NUMBER OF BONES THAT WERE BURIED?

7 THE CHIHUAHUA IS A BREED OF DOG THAT ORIGINATED IN WHAT COUNTRY?

8 HOW MANY WORDS ARE IN THE PREDICATE OF THE SENTENCE "MALACHI WALKS HIS DOG"?

9 BY DEFINITION, CYNOPHOBIA IS AN ABNORMAL FEAR OF WHAT?

DIGGING DINOSAURS

1

TRUE OR FALSE?
The Brachiosaurus was an herbivore.

2

Which of the following dinosaurs was a meat eater?
a. Brontosaurus
b. Tyrannosaurus
c. Stegosaurus

3

Which of these prehistoric animals could fly?
a. Triceratops
b. Pterodactyl
c. Velociraptor

4

TRUE OR FALSE?
Dinosaurs, some of which weighed 100 tons, were mammals.

5

Which of the following dinosaurs was the largest in size?

    a. Compsognathus
    b. Diplodocus
    c. Iguanodon

6

Theropod dinosaurs like the Allosaurus typically walked on how many legs?

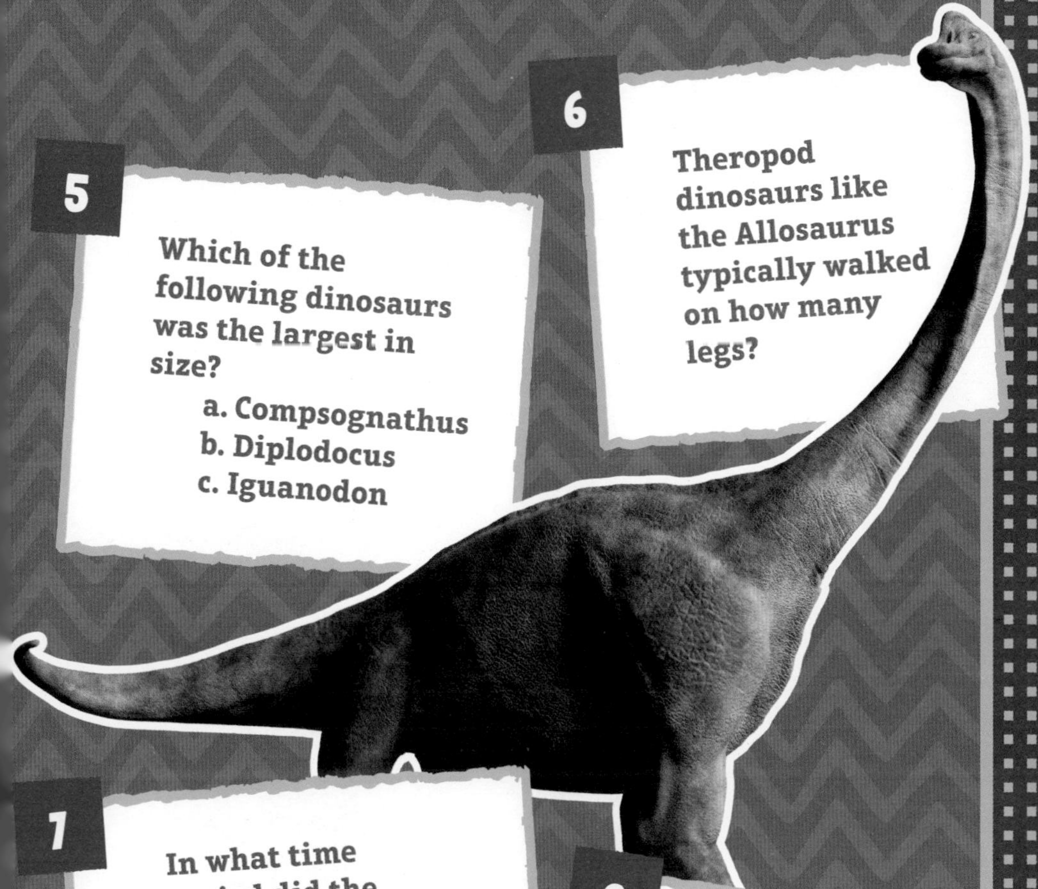

7

In what time period did the Tyrannosaurus rex roam the earth?

    a. Triassic
    b. Permian
    c. Cretaceous

8

TRUE OR FALSE?
All dinosaurs were carnivores.

9

The Mesozoic era was comprised of the Triassic period, the Cretaceous period, and what third geological period?

10

What era of geologic time is commonly referred to as the "age of dinosaurs"?

    a. Mesozoic
    b. Cenozoic
    c. Paleozoic

SUPER
SPACE

TO THE MOON AND BACK

1 What country's flag was the first to be placed on the moon?

2 Moonlight is light reflected off the moon's surface primarily from what source in our solar system?

3 TRUE OR FALSE? More light is reflected by the moon when it is in a gibbous as opposed to a crescent phase.

4 What type of eclipse occurs when the Earth is between the sun and the moon: solar or lunar?

5 What planet in our solar system has moons named Triton and Nereid?

6 Phobos and Deimos are moons that orbit which planet?

7

Callisto, Io, and Europa are all moons of Jupiter.

8

The second-largest moon in our solar system orbits Saturn. What is its name?

9

What planet in our solar system has over 25 known moons, including more than ten named for William Shakespeare characters?

10

What planet in our solar system has rings and a total of thirteen moons?

BONUS
WHAT IS THE NAME OF THE LARGEST MOON IN OUR SOLAR SYSTEM?

SEEING STARS

1. OUR SOLAR SYSTEM CONTAINS HOW MANY STARS?

2. KNOWN AS A "SHOOTING STAR," WHAT'S THE TERM FOR A PIECE OF ROCK OR METAL THAT BURNS BRIGHTLY IN THE SKY AS IT FALLS FROM OUTER SPACE?

    A. METEOR   B. COMET   C. ASTEROID

3. WHAT BRIGHT STAR IS THE FIRST STAR IN THE HANDLE OF THE LITTLE DIPPER CONSTELLATION?

4. WHICH OF THE FOLLOWING FORCES IS MOST RESPONSIBLE FOR THE FORMATION OF A NEW STAR?

    A. ENTROPY   B. GRAVITY   C. MAGNETISM

5. WHAT CONSTELLATION IN THE WINTER SKY GETS ITS NAME FROM THE LATIN WORD MEANING "BULL"?

6 MEANING "LITTLE BEAR" IN LATIN, WHAT CONSTELLATION CONTAINS THE GROUP OF STARS COMMONLY CALLED THE LITTLE DIPPER?

7 WHAT CONSTELLATION IS NAMED AFTER A MYTHICAL WINGED HORSE?

8 WHAT CONSTELLATION IN THE NORTHERN SKY, WHOSE NAME COMES FROM THE LATIN FOR "DRAGON," REPRESENTS THE CREATURE IN GREEK MYTHOLOGY WHO GUARDED THE GARDENS OF THE HESPERIDES?

9 WHAT STAR, LOCATED IN THE CONSTELLATION CANIS MAJOR, IS APPROXIMATELY 23 TIMES AS BRIGHT AS THE SUN?

THE PLANETS

5 Which planet in our solar system contains a massive storm nicknamed the Great Red Spot?

1 Which of the planets in our solar system has the most water?

6 What planet takes approximately 88 Earth days to revolve around the sun?

2 TRUE OR FALSE? Jupiter is so large that all the rest of the planets in our solar system could fit inside it.

3 Which planet in our solar system is fifth in distance from the sun?

7 Mercury is one of the two planets in our solar system that do not have a moon. What is the other?

4 TRUE OR FALSE? The volume of Jupiter is larger than the volumes of the other seven planets put together.

8 What planet in our solar system gets its name from the Roman king of the gods?

9 The dwarf planet Ceres orbits the sun in between the orbits of Mars and what other planet?

10 What is the only planet in our solar system that is named for a goddess?

11 How many planets in our solar system are considered Jovian planets?

12 In our solar system, the main asteroid belt exists between the orbit of Jupiter and the orbit of what other planet?

13 How many planets in our solar system have a circumference larger than Earth's?

14 Saturn's rings are primarily composed of which of the following?

    a. ammonia

    b. rocks and ice

    c. helium and other gases

15 How many planets in our solar system are classified as "gas giants"?

16 Which of the planets in our solar system was discovered in 1781 by British astronomer William Herschel?

17 Neptune takes about how many Earth years to complete one orbit around the sun?

    a. 16

    b. 165

    c. 212

18 **TRUE OR FALSE?**
The planet Uranus
has rings.

20 What is the
closest planet to
the sun to have a
natural satellite?

19 What is the only
planet in our
solar system that
rotates sideways
on its axis?

21 What planet in
our solar system
has the hottest
average surface
temperature?

SPACE EXPLORATION

1 In the initials of the federal agency NASA, what word does the letter "S" stand for?

2 While riding in a Mercury capsule, John Glenn became the first US astronaut to orbit what planet?

3 On July 20, 1976, NASA's Viking 1 was the first spacecraft to survive landing on the surface of which planet?

4 The first person to orbit Earth was from what country?

5 What was the name of the manned space station launched into space by NASA in 1973?

6 In 1965, what man aboard Gemini 4 became the first American to exit a spacecraft while it orbited Earth?

7 From the Latin for "twins," what was the name of NASA's second manned space program, which launched missions from 1964 to 1966?

BONUS WHAT WAS THE NAME AND NUMBER OF THE US SPACECRAFT THAT COMPLETED THE FIRST MANNED MISSION TO SEE THE FAR SIDE OF THE MOON?

8 The first mammal to be launched into space was from what species?

9 Michael Collins and Neil Armstrong were two of three astronauts on the famous Apollo 11 mission. Who was the third?

10 Apollo 17 was the last mission to land a man on the moon. In what year did it take place?

11 What was the name of the first satellite successfully launched into space in 1957?

BONUS IN 1961, WHAT MAN BECAME THE FIRST AMERICAN ASTRONAUT TO FLY INTO OUTER SPACE?

12 The name of NASA's first human spaceflight program shared its name with what planet?

BONUS WHAT WERE THE NAME AND NUMBER OF THE FIRST SPACECRAFT TO LAND ON THE MOON?

EARTH
ROCKS

1

BRUNO MARS LIVES ON WHICH LAYER OF EARTH?
A. CORE   B. MANTLE   C. CRUST

2

NOT COUNTING EARTH, WHAT IS THE ONLY CELESTIAL
BODY IN SPACE ON WHICH HUMANS HAVE WALKED?

3

WHAT IS THE NAME GIVEN TO ROCKS FALLING
TO EARTH FROM SPACE?
A. METEORITES   B. SATELLITES   C. NEBULAS

4

TRUE OR FALSE? WE ONLY EVER SEE ONE SIDE OF
THE MOON FROM EARTH.

5

THE OZONE LAYER IS LOCATED IN WHICH PART
OF EARTH'S ATMOSPHERE?
A. MESOSPHERE   B. STRATOSPHERE
C. THERMOSPHERE

6

WHAT IS THE SCIENTIFIC NAME OF THE OUTER
LAYER OF THE SUN NORMALLY VISIBLE
TO EARTH?
A. IONOSPHERE   B. PHOTOSPHERE
C. TROPOSPHERE

7

WHAT LAYER OF EARTH'S ATMOSPHERE
EXISTS BETWEEN THE STRATOSPHERE AND
THE THERMOSPHERE?

8

WHAT IS THE SECOND MOST COMMON ELEMENT
IN EARTH'S ATMOSPHERE?

BONUS WHAT
LAYER OF EARTH
LIES DIRECTLY
UNDERNEATH THE
LITHOSPHERE?

BONUS TO
THE NEAREST
MINUTE, HOW
LONG DOES
IT TAKE FOR
LIGHT TO
REACH EARTH
FROM THE
SUN?

THE SOLAR SYSTEM

1. **TRUE OR FALSE?** A planet's orbit around the sun is always a perfect circle.

2. Our solar system is located in what galaxy?

3. If Kanye West were standing at the equator, what direction would he face in order to watch the sun set?
   - a. west
   - b. east
   - c. kanyeast

4. By definition, a lunar calendar is based on the movements of what celestial body?

5. **TRUE OR FALSE?** By definition, asteroids orbit planets.

6. The orbits of how many planets lie between the orbit of Earth and the sun?

7. What object in our solar system has a surface temperature of approximately 10,800 degrees Fahrenheit?

8. **TRUE OR FALSE?** The sun is located in the center of the universe.

9. By definition, which of the following terms describes one full journey of Earth around the sun?
   - a. eclipse
   - b. revolution
   - c. rotation

10. Which of the following cannot be found in our solar system?
    - a. constellations
    - b. comets
    - c. asteroids

11. What celestial object in our solar system is named for the Roman god of the underworld and was first discovered in 1930?

12 By definition, meteors are blocks of rock and ice that break off from which of the following celestial bodies?

   a. asteroids

   b. planets

   c. stars

13 Approximately how long does it take the sun to make one revolution around the Milky Way galaxy?

   a. 52 weeks

   b. 325,000 years

   c. 250 million years

14 Earth circles the sun in approximately 365 days. Which planet in our solar system takes approximately 687 Earth days to circle the sun?

15 Along with the moon, what other celestial object in our solar system most affects Earth's tides?

16 In terms of size, place the following in order from smallest to largest: Milky Way galaxy, universe, solar system.

17 By mass, the sun is made primarily of what element?

18 Which layer of the sun is closest to its core?

   a. corona

   b. chromosphere

   c. photosphere

19 What is the maximum number of times per century Halley's Comet can be seen with the naked eye from Earth?

20 The Milky Way is the second-largest galaxy in a group of galaxies known as the Local Group. What is the largest?

21 From the Latin for "mist," what is the word for a cloud of gas or dust that occurs in interstellar space?

BONUS HALLEY'S COMET IS SLATED TO BECOME VISIBLE FROM EARTH NEXT DURING WHAT DECADE?

EXPLORE THE USA

US PRESIDENTS

1 What US president commissioned the 19th-century cross-country expedition led by explorers Meriwether Lewis and William Clark?

2 All of the first six US presidents came either from Virginia or what other US state?

    a. Massachusetts

    b. New York

    c. Pennsylvania

3 Mount Vernon, the home of US president George Washington, is located in what state?

4 How many men served as US president during the 18th century?

BONUS THE FEDERAL RESERVE SYSTEM WAS INSTITUTED UNDER THE ADMINISTRATION OF WHAT US PRESIDENT?

5 Awarded to US soldiers, the Purple Heart features the image of which US president?

    a. George Washington

    b. Herbert Hoover

    c. Richard Nixon

6 Abraham Lincoln was the first man to be elected US president as a member of which political party?

7 Who was the youngest person to be elected president of the US?

8 In which of the thirteen original colonies was US president George Washington born?

9 Among the men featured on the Mount Rushmore National Memorial, who was the first to be president of the US?

10 Which of the following was not created under President Franklin D. Roosevelt's New Deal?

    a. Internal Revenue Service

    b. Securities and Exchange Commission

    c. Social Security system

BONUS IN ONE OF THE MOST IMPORTANT ELECTIONS IN US HISTORY, ABRAHAM LINCOLN WAS ELECTED PRESIDENT IN 1860. WHO WAS HIS VICE PRESIDENT?

11 Who was the first US president to be inaugurated in Washington, DC?

12 There are four US presidents who served without a vice president the entire time they were in office. John Tyler, Millard Fillmore, and Andrew Johnson are three. Who is the fourth?

13 "O captain, my captain! Our fearful trip is done," is the first line of a poem by Walt Whitman, which he wrote to honor the memory of what US president?

14 What is the first and last name of the man who served as US president longer than any other person?

15 Nicknamed "the father of the Constitution," what future US president introduced the Bill of Rights to Congress in 1789?

16 Calvin Coolidge was the vice president under which US president?

BONUS WHO WAS THE LAST MAN TO SERVE AS US PRESIDENT AS A MEMBER OF THE WHIG PARTY?

17 Aaron Burr served as vice president during the administration of which US president?

18 Nicknamed "Old Rough and Ready," what general who fought in the Mexican-American War went on to become a US president in 1849?

19 What US president began a series of legislative initiatives known as the New Frontier in 1961?

20 Who was the only US president to be a member of the army in both World War I and World War II?

21 In 1933, what US president began giving a series of speeches on the radio known as "fireside chats"?

22 The 21st US president was President Arthur. What was his first name?

23 What US president had the campaign slogan "I Like Ike"?

24 TRUE OR FALSE? Benjamin Franklin was secretary of state for US president George Washington.

25 What US president founded and designed the layout of the University of Virginia?

BONUS WHO WAS THE FIRST MAN TO BECOME US PRESIDENT WITHOUT BEING ELECTED TO THAT OFFICE?

26 Who was US president immediately before Abraham Lincoln?

27 What US president first popularized the phrase "Speak softly and carry a big stick" when talking about his approach to foreign policy?

28 Who was the US president when the first person walked on the moon?

29 Who was the first woman to be both the wife and mother of a US president?

30 Three vice presidents served under US president Franklin D. Roosevelt. John Nance Garner and Henry A. Wallace are two. Who was the third?

31 Who was the only US president to have earned a PhD before taking office?

32 US president George Washington was born in 1732. In what year did he die?

33 In order to be president of the United States, a person must be at least how many years of age?

34 What US vice president resigned in 1832 and went on to become a senator from South Carolina?

35 The Rough Riders was the name given to the first United States volunteer cavalry, whose members included what future US president?

36 What man renamed the official US presidential retreat Camp David, after his grandson?

BONUS WHO WAS THE FIRST MAN TO BE US PRESIDENT WHEN THE US HAD FIFTY STATES?

THE FIFTY STATES

1. What ocean surrounds the US state of Hawaii?

2. What is the only US state whose name begins with the letter "D"?

3. Occupying over 2 million square feet, the Metropolitan Museum of Art is located in what US city?

4. **TRUE OR FALSE?** Tallahassee, Florida, is the southernmost US state capital.

5. Four US states have names that begin and end with the same letter. Alabama, Alaska, and Arizona are three. What is the fourth?

6. **TRUE OR FALSE?** If Danielle is standing on the east coast of Asia, she can dive into the Pacific Ocean.

7. What is the only US state that has territory above the Arctic Circle?

8. With an official elevation of 5,280 feet, what US city of around 600,000 people is known as the Mile High City?

9. Which of the following US states borders both South Dakota and Illinois?

   a. Iowa

   b. Minnesota

   c. Wisconsin

10. What US state is home to a chain of islands known as the Keys?

11. Olympic National Park is located in what US state?

BONUS HOW MANY US STATES SHARE A LAND BORDER WITH CANADA?

12 What national park comprises the largest subtropical wilderness in the United States?

13 What library located in Washington, DC, has over 33 million books?

14 What US state is nicknamed "the Land of Lincoln"?

BONUS SOME OF THE HIGHEST SAND DUNES IN THE US ARE LOCATED IN GREAT SAND DUNES NATIONAL PARK AND PRESERVE. IN WHAT STATE IS IT LOCATED?

17 Knoxville is one of the most populous cities in what US state that lies immediately north of Alabama?

15 If you're on a road trip and traveling to the capital of North Dakota, then you're on your way to what city?

16 What is the only letter of the alphabet that does not appear in the name of a US state?

18 From 1910 to 1940, Angel Island served as the port of entry into the US for thousands of Asian immigrants. Angel Island is part of what US state?

BONUS DECLARED A NATIONAL MONUMENT IN 1908, THE NATURAL BRIDGES ARE LOCATED IN WHAT US STATE?

21 Idaho is bordered by how many states?

22 What state borders North Dakota to the west?

19 New York City is made up of five boroughs. Manhattan, Queens, the Bronx, and Brooklyn are four of them. What is the fifth?

23 Name two of the four states that border Texas.

24 The Great Smoky Mountains National Park is located in two US states. Name both of them.

20 Mississippi is one of two states that have three pairs of side-by-side double letters in their names. What is the other state?

25 What US state is home to Theodore Roosevelt National Park?

26 Authorized by Thomas Jefferson, the Cumberland Road ultimately followed which of the following routes?

    a. Georgia to Oklahoma

    b. Maryland to Illinois

    c. New York to Michigan

27 Mark Twain National Forest is located in what US state?

28 In terms of surface area, which of the Great Lakes is the smallest?

29 What US state is home to the Kenai National Wildlife Refuge?

30 What is the only US state that borders only one other US state?

31 How many other US states border Tennessee?

32 What US state capital is the highest in elevation?

33 The largest facility that produces electrical power in the US, the Grand Coulee Dam, is located in which state?

BONUS WHAT CITY WAS FOUNDED IN 1610, MAKING IT THE OLDEST CITY TO CURRENTLY SERVE AS A US STATE CAPITAL?

HISTORY

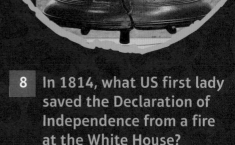

1. The White House is located on what avenue in Washington, DC?

2. **TRUE OR FALSE?** New Jersey was one of the original thirteen colonies.

3. What are the last five words in the US Pledge of Allegiance?

4. What Washington, DC, memorial, dedicated in 1922, is named in honor of the 16th US president?

5. What city has been the capital of the United States for over 200 years?

6. The sugar maple is the official tree for what US state that entered the Union in 1791?

7. Colorado is nicknamed "the Centennial State" because it became a US state in what year?

8. In 1814, what US first lady saved the Declaration of Independence from a fire at the White House?

9. **TRUE OR FALSE?** The Liberty Bell in Philadelphia cracked in 1776 and was never rung again.

10. Plymouth Rock, the site where the Pilgrims landed in 1620, is located in what US state?

    a. Virginia

    b. Massachusetts

    c. New Hampshire

11. What is the only US state whose name starts with two vowels?

12 The pua aloalo is the official flower of what US state?

13 Fill in the blank from the Declaration of Independence: "We hold these _____ to be self-evident."

14 Dedicated in 1922, what US national monument in Washington, DC, contains the Gettysburg Address engraved on a stone tablet?

15 How many of the thirteen original colonies had the word "new" in their name?

16 Designed and lived in by US president Thomas Jefferson, what estate, over 200 years old, is located in Virginia?

17 TRUE OR FALSE? In the Revolutionary War, the Battle of Lexington took place on the same day as the Battle of Concord.

BONUS "DON'T FIRE 'TIL YOU SEE THE WHITES OF THEIR EYES" WERE THE WORDS ATTRIBUTED TO CAPTAIN ISRAEL PUTNAM AT WHAT REVOLUTIONARY WAR BATTLE?

18 The land comprising the modern state of Florida was purchased from what country in 1819?

19 Which of the following US states has the longest freshwater shoreline?

a. California

b. Florida

c. Michigan

20 "Eureka" is the motto of what US state?

21 What US naval base, the headquarters of the Pacific fleet, was attacked by Japan on December 7, 1941?

22 The original Pony Express was a rapid postal system in the US by which mail was delivered by riders on horseback. In what century did it operate?

23 Which of these US states was one of the original thirteen colonies?

a. Ohio

b. Alabama

c. North Carolina

24 Which of the following monuments is tallest?

a. Gateway Arch

b. Statue of Liberty

c. Washington Monument

25 Paul Revere's famous midnight ride, in which he warned that the British were coming, took place on what date in 1775?

26 In what present-day US state can you find the abandoned cliff dwellings of the Anasazi people?

    a. Colorado

    b. Hawaii

    c. Vermont

27 During what war did Francis Scott Key pen "The Star-Spangled Banner?"

28 Known as "the Volunteer State," what was the 16th US state to join the Union?

29 The battles of Saratoga, which took place during the US Revolutionary War, occurred in what present-day US state?

30 Which of the original thirteen American colonies was founded by philanthropist James Oglethorpe?

31 What Native American, who lived with the Wampanoag tribe, served as chief interpreter and guide to Pilgrim William Bradford?

32 Now a national historical park, what site was headquarters for George Washington's army in the winter of 1777–78?

33 Immediately before joining the Union in 1820, Maine was part of which other US state?

34 The Louisiana Purchase, which more than doubled the area of the United States, was made in what year?

35 In what year did the US Civil War officially end?

BONUS WHICH WAS THE LAST OF THE ORIGINAL THIRTEEN AMERICAN COLONIES TO RATIFY THE US CONSTITUTION?

36 In 1898, during the administration of President William McKinley, an explosion aboard the US battleship *Maine* ignited a war between the US and what country?

37 During the gold rush, many settlers moved west along a route known as the California Trail. One of the main branches of the trail ended at Sutter's Fort in what city?

BONUS DURING THE CIVIL WAR, HOW MANY TOTAL STATES SECEDED FROM THE UNION?

38 Which of the original thirteen US states refused to take part in the Constitutional Convention of 1787?

39 On May 10, 1869, the first transcontinental railroad was officially completed when the last spike was driven into the ground in what present-day US state?

40 If you were taking a field trip to the US state named for a French king, then you'd be heading to what state?

41 In what city did the Second Continental Congress meet in 1775?

42 What southern US state is the only state whose legal system comes from the Napoleonic Code?

43 In 1777, the Continental Army set up camp at Valley Forge in what present-day US state?

44 Who was US president when the United Nations was officially formed?

45 Known as "the Great Compromiser," Senator Henry Clay represented what state in Congress during the 1800s?

46 In 1916, more than three years before women had the right to vote, what female from Montana became the first woman elected to the US Congress?

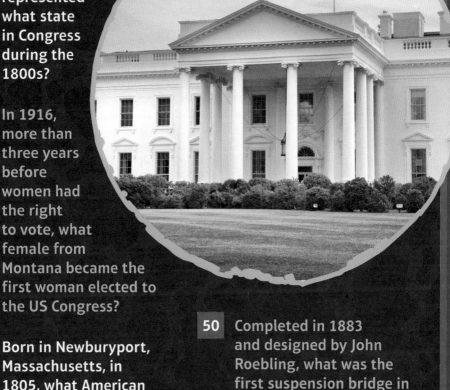

47 Born in Newburyport, Massachusetts, in 1805, what American abolitionist and journalist founded the newspaper called *The Liberator*?

48 What man received a majority of the popular vote in the US presidential election of 1876 but did not become president?

49 At the beginning of the US Civil War, what state was the first to officially secede from the Union?

50 Completed in 1883 and designed by John Roebling, what was the first suspension bridge in the US to use steel for its cable wire?

51 Famous for saving the life of Captain John Smith, Pocahontas was the daughter of what Indian chief?

BONUS THE WORLD'S HIGHEST SUSPENSION BRIDGE, THE ROYAL GORGE BRIDGE IS LOCATED IN WHAT US STATE?

US GOVERNMENT

1. US presidential elections always occur on what day of the week?

2. **TRUE OR FALSE?** Thomas Jefferson is featured on the face of the nickel.

3. What is the official name for the federal holiday celebrated on July 4th?
   - a. Flag Day
   - b. Independence Day
   - c. Patriot Day

4. How many chief justices serve on the US Supreme Court?

5. The majority of US coins are made in which of the following places?
   - a. the White House
   - b. the US Mint
   - c. the Library of Congress

6. What amendment to the US Constitution guarantees freedom of speech and the press?

BONUS RESULTING IN PROHIBITION, WHICH AMENDMENT TO THE US CONSTITUTION BANNED THE MANUFACTURE, TRANSPORTATION, AND SALE OF ALCOHOL?

7. What building in Washington, DC, serves as the official meeting place for the US Congress?

8. **TRUE OR FALSE?** If there's a tie in the electoral college in a US presidential election, the Senate holds a vote to decide who will be the president.

9. **TRUE OR FALSE?** A bill in the US House of Representatives can only be introduced by a member of the House.

10 Which amendment in the Bill of Rights protects American citizens against cruel and unusual punishment?

11 The headquarters of the US Department of Defense, the Pentagon is located in what US state?

12 Which part of the US Constitution describes how it can be amended?

　a. the Articles

　b. the Bill of Rights

　c. the Preamble

13 In the US presidential oath of office, the president swears to "preserve, protect and defend" what document?

14 Which of the following US historical documents, written in 1787, begins with a short statement called the Preamble?

　a. US Constitution

　b. Declaration of Independence

　c. Gettysburg Address

15 The presidential Cabinet is a part of which of the three main branches of the federal government?

16 The legislative branch of the US government has a bicameral structure, which means it has how many chambers?

17 According to Article 5 of the US Constitution, which branch of the US federal government has the power to "propose Amendments to this Constitution"?

    a. legislative

    b. executive

    c. judicial

BONUS WHAT 1803 US SUPREME COURT CASE ESTABLISHED THE PRECEDENT OF JUDICIAL REVIEW?

18 In the US army, which of the following officer classes ranks the highest?

    a. captain

    b. lieutenant

    c. major

19 In the US federal government, what member of the executive branch appoints US federal judges?

    a. the president

    b. the attorney general

    c. the chief justice of the Supreme Court

20 TRUE OR FALSE? George Washington was one of the signers of the US Constitution.

21 Which of the following is not one of the three branches of the US federal government?

    a. judicial

    b. military

    c. legislative

22 Which branch of the US armed services was formed most recently?

23 In the US navy, what rank is immediately superior to a commander?

24 The Supreme Court falls under which of the three branches of the US government?

25 If the vote is tied in the US Senate, what government official casts the tie-breaking vote?

26 TRUE OR FALSE? Decisions handed down by the US Supreme Court can be appealed.

27 Number One Observatory Circle is the official residence for which of the following?

    a. director of the CIA

    b. secretary of state

    c. vice president

BONUS THE TEXT OF THE 20TH AMENDMENT TO THE US CONSTITUTION STATES THAT CONGRESS SHALL MEET AT LEAST ONCE A YEAR AND SUCH MEETING SHALL BE ON WHAT DATE?

28 Which of the following historical documents was the last to be ratified?

    a. Articles of Confederation

    b. Bill of Rights

    c. Declaration of Independence

29 Washington, DC, was given electoral votes as a result of the 23rd Amendment to the US Constitution. How many electoral votes does Washington, DC, have?

30 According to Article 5 of the US Constitution, what percentage of the states must ratify a Constitutional amendment for it to take effect?

31 What act of Parliament in 1765 taxed American colonists by requiring them to buy specific types of paper for newspapers, bills of sale, and wills?

32 Which amendment in the Bill of Rights states that rights not defined in the Constitution are still protected?

33 Benjamin Franklin signed the Declaration of Independence as a representative from which new state?

34 Which branch of Congress must approve the nomination of a US Supreme Court justice?

35 Which amendment in the US Bill of Rights prohibits unreasonable search and seizure without a warrant?

36 According to Article 1, Section 3, of the US Constitution, to become a US senator a person must have been a US citizen for at least how many years?

37 What lawyer who argued before the US Supreme Court in *Brown v. Board of Education of Topeka* later became a Supreme Court justice himself?

38 What document that preceded the Constitution gave Congress the authority to govern the United States between 1781 and 1789?

39 Shays' Rebellion, which made lawmakers realize they needed a stronger central government, originated in what US state in the 1780s?

40 The federal agency that oversees much of our public lands is called the BLM. What does BLM stand for?

41 What Cabinet position appointed by the president is the chief law enforcement officer of the US federal government?

42 The original Bill of Rights is located in what building found in Washington, DC?

43 If a US president is impeached and all 100 senators are voting, how many votes are needed to remove him/her from office?

BONUS WHAT AMENDMENT TO THE US CONSTITUTION GRANTS WOMEN THE RIGHT TO VOTE IN FEDERAL ELECTIONS?

ARTS & CULTURE

WORKS OF ART

1 Which of the following is a three-dimensional art form in which miniatures are displayed in a shoebox?
  a. crochet
  b. diorama
  c. embroidery

2 If Quinne has a jar of blue paint, a jar of red paint, and a jar of yellow paint, how many secondary colors can she create?

3 The Leonardo da Vinci painting known as the *Mona Lisa* hangs in what museum?

4 On a color wheel, what color is complementary to violet?

6 The *Ginevra de' Benci*, the only publicly displayed Leonardo da Vinci painting in the United States, is located in the National Gallery of Art in what US city?

5 Named for an 18th-century French finance minister, what type of artwork involves making an outline of an object and then filling it in with a solid color?

7 Painter Georgia O'Keeffe, famous for her depictions of flowers and landscapes, was born in what country?

8 In the 16th century, what artist painted the ceiling of the Sistine Chapel?

9 What Dutch artist born in 1853 is famous for his paintings *Irises*, *Sunflowers*, and *The Potato Eaters*?

10 Renaissance artist and inventor Leonardo da Vinci was born in 1452 in what modern-day country?

11 What artist known for his sketches of birds gave his name to a wildlife foundation first formed in 1905?

12 Seen in Florence, Italy, since 1504, Michelangelo's famous statue is named for what biblical hero?

14 The 17th-century artist Rembrandt, known for his painting *The Night Watch*, was born in what present-day European country?

13 What famous portrait by Leonardo da Vinci is also known as *La Gioconda*?

15 Renowned artists Pablo Picasso and Salvador Dalí were born in what country?

16 Founded in 1764, the Hermitage is an art museum located in what Russian city?

BOOKS, BOOKS, BOOKS

1   In A. A. Milne's classic books, what is the name of the human boy who goes on adventures with Winnie the Pooh?

2   The classic Hans Christian Andersen fairy tale "The Real Princess" is better known as "The Princess and the . . ." what?

3   Born in the 1780s, the Brothers Grimm are best known for which of the following?
    a. songs
    b. fairy tales
    c. tweets

4   In what classic children's book does the title character arrive to Earth from an asteroid and fall in love with a rose?
    a. *The Little Prince*
    b. *A Cricket in Times Square*
    c. *James and the Giant Peach*

5   The classic E. B. White novel *Charlotte's Web* centers on a spider named Charlotte and a pig named what?

6   What ancient Greek storyteller is credited with creating fables such as "The Tortoise and the Hare" and "The Boy Who Cried Wolf"?

7   If Isabella reads exactly 5 books every month, how many books will she read in a year?

8 In the legendary Aesop fable, the fox tries in vain to reach what fruit?

9 First published in 1908, what classic children's book by Kenneth Grahame featured the characters Rat, Mole, Toad, and Badger?

10 What French author wrote the classic 1844 novel *The Three Musketeers*?

11 What American author wrote *The Adventures of Tom Sawyer*?

12 What fictional detective is the main character of many Arthur Conan Doyle works, including *The Hound of the Baskervilles*?

13 First published in the 1800s, what short story written by Washington Irving is named for a character who falls asleep underneath a tree for 20 years?

14 In 1731, what man founded the first American public library, which was located in Philadelphia?

15 Poet Walt Whitman wrote *Leaves of Grass* in 1855. What country was he born in?

16 In the Charles Dickens story "A Christmas Carol," what is the first name of the main character, who has the last name Scrooge?

17 First published in the US in 1882, what book by Mark Twain set in 16th-century England tells the story of two strangers who look identical and decide to switch places?

18 What British author wrote the 1813 novel *Pride and Prejudice?*

19 What Shakespeare play features the characters Iago and Desdemona?

20 What 1956 novel by Fred Gipson tells the story of brothers Arliss and Travis and the big dog who befriends and protects them?

21 Set in Alaska, the 1903 novel *The Call of the Wild* tells the story of a dog named Buck who works as a sled dog in the Klondike gold rush. What American author wrote the novel?

22 The line, "To be or not to be, that is the question," is spoken by the title character in what Shakespearean play?

23 What book series is based on Laura Ingalls Wilder's 19th-century life on the American frontier?

24 What classic children's novel begins with a character named Fern asking, "Where's papa going with that ax?"

25 Which of these is a book by author Jonathan Swift?

    a. *Gulliver's Travels*

    b. *Treasure Island*

    c. *My Sister, Taylor Swift*

BONUS WHAT AMERICAN AUTHOR WROTE THE STORIES "THE TELL-TALE HEART" AND "THE PIT AND THE PENDULUM"?

26 In Washington Irving's story "The Legend of Sleepy Hollow," is Ichabod Crane the protagonist or antagonist?

27 First published in 1838, the novel *Oliver Twist* follows the story of an orphan who meets a gang of pickpockets in London. Who is the author of that novel?

28 Shakespeare's *Romeo and Juliet* features two feuding families. One was the Capulets; what was the other?

29 First published as a book in 1883, the classic children's novel *Treasure Island* was written by what author?

30 What American poet, born in 1874, authored the poem "Stopping by Woods on a Snowy Evening"?

31 In *The Iliad*, Aphrodite gets Paris to decree her the most beautiful immortal in exchange for the love of which woman?

32 Isabella's favorite book is the 1850 novel *David Copperfield*. Who wrote it?

33 What book by Harper Lee features the characters Scout, Atticus, and Boo Radley?

34 What book by Frances Hodgson Burnett tells the story of Mary Lennox, a girl who discovers and rehabilitates a flower patch?

35 *The Last of the Mohicans* is a novel that tells the story of Uncas, a noble Native American who helps a settler family. Who wrote the novel?

36 In what novel by Jonathan Swift would you find townspeople called "Lilliputians" and creatures called "Yahoos"?

37 What British author wrote *The Canterbury Tales* in the 14th century?

38 What 19th-century female poet born in Amherst, Massachusetts, wrote the poem "I'm Nobody! Who are you?"

39 Shakespeare wrote many of his sonnets in iambic pentameter, a rhyming scheme in which each line consists of how many syllables?

40 How many lines of verse does a Shakespearean sonnet contain?

41 First published in 1873, the novel *Around the World in Eighty Days* was written by which author?

42 What 1937 novel by J. R. R. Tolkien tells the story of Bilbo Baggins and his quest for the treasure guarded by a dragon, Smaug?

43 The original novel *Frankenstein* was composed in the early 19th century by what female British writer?

44 First published in 1847, the novel *Jane Eyre* was written by what female English author?

45 What novel by Charles Dickens begins "It was the best of times, it was the worst of times"?

46 What 1850 novel by Nathaniel Hawthorne tells the story of Hester Prynne and Arthur Dimmesdale?

47 A short story about a mongoose and two cobras, "Rikki Tikki Tavi" was a story that first appeared in *The Jungle Book*, by which British author?

48 According to William Shakespeare, "Et tu, Brute?" were the last words of what famous Roman leader?

49 First published in 1812, what classic children's novel by Johann Wyss tells the story of a family shipwrecked in the South Seas?

50 In Sir Arthur Conan Doyle's classic book series, what friend of Sherlock Holmes narrates most of the stories, including *A Study in Scarlet*?

51 What is the name of the 14th-century Italian author who wrote *Inferno*, which was part of his epic poem *The Divine Comedy*?

52 The English author who published the *Peter Rabbit* books starting in 1902 had the first name Beatrix. What was her last name?

BONUS WTHE STORY OF SCHOOLBOYS STRANDED ON A DESERTED ISLAND, *LORD OF THE FLIES* WAS WRITTEN BY WHICH AUTHOR?

53 Which American author who was a key part of the Harlem Renaissance published collections of poems including *The First Book of Jazz*?

54 What 1925 novel by F. Scott Fitzgerald features the characters Nick Carraway and Daisy Buchanan?

55 First published in the 1880s, what story by Mark Twain features a resident of Hartford who time travels back to medieval England?

56 "The Little Mermaid" and "The Little Match Girl" are stories written by what Danish author?

MUSIC CLASS

1 Which of the following vocal parts sings the lowest?

    a. alto

    b. bass

    c. tenor

2 In the song "She'll Be Comin' 'Round the Mountain," how many white horses will she be drivin' when she comes?

3 How many 16th notes equals one quarter note?

4 A basic musical staff is composed of 4 spaces and how many lines?

5 In the 1936 orchestral piece *Peter and the Wolf*, what instrument traditionally represents the bird?

    a. clarinet

    b. flute

    c. trumpet

6 If Mia is performing in a quartet, by definition how many other performers are there besides her?

7 If a musical piece is written in ¾ time, how many beats are there per measure?

8 Chloe sings in the school choir. If she is in the group with the highest female vocal range, then she is in which of the following groups?

    a. sopranos

    b. altos

    c. baritones

9 The Grand Ole Opry, a weekly country music stage concert begun in 1925, is located in what US state?

10 Tchaikovsky, famous for composing the ballets *Swan Lake* and *The Nutcracker*, was born in what country?

11 A single lowercase letter "f" represents what Italian word that instructs musicians to play loudly?

12 How many 8th notes make up a half note?

13 With music by Tchaikovsky, what ballet first performed in 1890 tells the story of a princess who falls asleep for 100 years when she pricks her finger on a spindle?

14 On a staff, musical notes are identified by how many letters in the alphabet?

15 Which American folk singer born in 1912 wrote and recorded the classic song "This Land Is Your Land"?

16 What opera by Rossini tells the story of a Swiss patriot who shoots an arrow through an apple on his son's head?

LET'S MAKE MUSIC

1 TRUE OR FALSE? THE MUSICAL INSTRUMENT KNOWN AS A RECORDER IS A MEMBER OF THE WOODWIND FAMILY.

2 THE TROMBONE, TRUMPET, AND TUBA ARE ALL MEMBERS OF WHAT FAMILY OF MUSICAL INSTRUMENTS?

3 THE FIDDLE IS ANOTHER NAME FOR WHICH OF THE FOLLOWING INSTRUMENTS?
A. VIOLIN   B. TRIANGLE   C. TRUMPET

4 WHICH OF THE FOLLOWING IS USED AS A PART OF CLARINETS, OBOES, AND BASSOONS TO HELP MAKE THEIR SOUND?
A. REED   B. CHIME   C. SLIDE

5 WHAT PERCUSSION INSTRUMENT SHARES ITS NAME WITH A THREE-SIDED GEOMETRIC SHAPE?

6 TRUE OR FALSE? THE FRENCH HORN, THE TRUMPET, AND THE XYLOPHONE ARE ALL IN THE SAME MUSICAL FAMILY.

7 A MODERN STANDARD PIANO HAS WHICH OF THE FOLLOWING?
A. MORE WHITE KEYS THAN BLACK KEYS
B. MORE BLACK KEYS THAN WHITE KEYS
C. EQUAL NUMBER OF WHITE AND BLACK KEYS

8 THE BAGPIPE IS THE NATIONAL INSTRUMENT OF WHAT COUNTRY THAT IS PART OF THE UNITED KINGDOM?

9 WHICH OF THE FOLLOWING IS AN INSTRUMENT IN THE WOODWIND FAMILY?
A. VIOLIN   B. SAXOPHONE
C. TRUMPET

10 TRUE OR FALSE? MARACAS ARE PERCUSSION INSTRUMENTS.

11 CASTANETS BELONG TO WHICH OF THE FOLLOWING MUSICAL FAMILIES?
A. BRASS   B. PERCUSSION   C. WOODWIND

12

WHICH OF THE FOLLOWING
WOODWIND INSTRUMENTS IS
TYPICALLY DEEPEST IN PITCH?
A. BASSOON
B. CLARINET
C. OBOE

13

IF THREE OF YOUR
FANS ARE IN THE
STANDS PLAYING A
TOM-TOM, A BONGO,
AND A SNARE, WHAT
TYPE OF MUSICAL
INSTRUMENT ARE
THEY ALL PLAYING?

14

THE HARP IS A MEMBER
OF WHICH OF THE FOLLOWING
MUSICAL FAMILIES?
A. PERCUSSION
B. WOODWIND
C. STRINGS

15

A GONG IS TO A MALLET AS A VIOLIN
IS TO WHICH OF THE FOLLOWING?
A. BOW   B. DRUMSTICK   C. OBOE

16

FROM THE ITALIAN FOR "SMALL," WHAT IS THE WORD FOR THE MINIATURE FLUTE THAT PLAYS AN OCTAVE HIGHER THAN AN ORDINARY FLUTE?

17

BY DEFINITION, A SOUSAPHONE IS A VARIATION OF WHAT LARGE BRASS INSTRUMENT?

18

TRUE OR FALSE?
A HARPSICHORD IS AN EXAMPLE OF A WOODWIND INSTRUMENT.

19

WHICH INSTRUMENT IS THE LOWEST-PITCHED MEMBER OF THE VIOLIN FAMILY?
A. CELLO   B. VIOLA   C. DOUBLE BASS

20

KNOWN FOR ITS DOUBLE REED, WHAT INSTRUMENT DO ALL THE OTHER INSTRUMENTS IN THE ORCHESTRA TYPICALLY TUNE TO?

21

IN A MODERN ORCHESTRA, THE "CONCERTMASTER" IS TYPICALLY THE FIRST-CHAIR MUSICIAN OF WHAT INSTRUMENT?

22

THE OBOE IS A MEMBER OF WHAT FAMILY OF INSTRUMENTS?

THE MUSIC SHOW

1 The 17th-century composer Antonio Vivaldi, famous for the *Four Seasons* concertos, was born in what modern-day country?

2 What famous composer, born in Salzburg, Austria, in 1756, wrote over 600 works?

3 Which of the following composers continued to write music even after he became completely deaf?
a. Beethoven
b. Bach
c. Mozart

4 Known for his marches, which American composer wrote "The Stars and Stripes Forever"?

5 What Russian-born composer wrote the music for the 1913 ballet *The Rite of Spring*?

6 American composer George Gershwin, who wrote the 1924 piece *Rhapsody in Blue*, often worked with his brother, who was a lyricist. What was his brother's name?

7 The music to the opera *The Magic Flute* was written by what 18th-century composer?

8 Not counting unfinished works, classical composer Ludwig van Beethoven wrote a total of how many symphonies during his life?

9 Born in 1685, J. S. Bach was one of the greatest composers in the history of music. What do the initials J. S. stand for?

10 "The Dance of the Sugar Plum Fairy" occurs in what ballet with music by Tchaikovsky?

11 In the 18th century, what German musician composed the *Brandenburg Concertos*?

BACK TO SCHOOL

GRAMMAR & ENGLISH

1 Which of the following parts of speech is not necessary to form a sentence?

   a. adjective   b. noun

   c. verb

2 **TRUE OR FALSE?** There are no words in the English language that contain four different vowels.

3 How many common nouns are in the following rhyme? "Humpty Dumpty sat on a wall, Humpty Dumpty had a big fall."

4 What part of speech is the word "twirled" in the following sentence? "Saya and Patrick twirled their hula hoops."

5 In English, which of these prefixes typically means "not"?

   a. de b. im c. meta

6 What word in the following sentence is an antonym of "tiny"? "The tiny mouse helped the enormous elephant to open the door."

7 Which of the following words can be used as both a verb and a noun?

   a. avoid

   b. drive

   c. told

8 Which of the following is a homophone for the word "know"?

   a. ignorant   b. no

   c. understand

9 Which of the following sentences is an example of a simile?

   a. Amira loves jumbo shrimp.

   b. Cooper slept like a bear.

   c. Quinne writes right.

10 The phrase "I almost died laughing" is an example of which of the following?

   a. alliteration

   b. hyperbole

   c. palindrome

11 "Jamir jumped joyfully" is an example of which of the following?

   a. simile

   b. palindrome

   c. alliteration

12 What word in the following sentence is a palindrome? "Chloe paddled her kayak swiftly down the stream."

13 Which of the following is an anagram of the word "add"?

    a. adding

    b. dad

    c. subtract

14 Which of these is an example of hyperbole?

    a. A man, a plan, a canal, Panama.

    b. Tristan is so hungry, he could eat a horse.

    c. The cars vroomed past us.

15 Which of the following words can be an adjective?

    a. poor

    b. pore

    c. pour

16 How many common nouns are in this sentence?

17 Words with identical spellings that have different meanings and pronunciations are known as which of the following?

    a. heteronyms

    b. synonyms

    c. homonyms

18 Which of the following is an example of alliteration?

    a. Hey, you!

    b. The rain in Spain

    c. Pretty please

19 **TRUE OR FALSE?** In grammar, a diphthong refers to two consonants that are pronounced as one syllable.

20 Which of the following words is an example of an acronym?

    a. antimatter

    b. boom

    c. radar

21 Which of the followings phrases is an example of a split infinitive?

    a. be all that you can be

    b. carefully follow through

    c. to boldly go

22 How many prepositions are in the following sentence? "After school, Nick jumped in a lake because it was a hot day."

23 How many singular possessive nouns are there in the following sentence? "After Colin's cat ate the children's lunches, he licked his whiskers."

MATH SKILLS

1 x plus 0 always equals what number?

2 What is the greatest integer between 1 and 100 to have a 7 in the tens place?

3 If Patrick breaks his piggy bank and finds $1.05 worth of nickels, how many nickels does he have?

4 How many odd numbers are there between the numbers 16 and 26?

5 How many tens are in the number 65?

6 What is the lowest positive integer?

7 What three-digit whole number has a 7 in the ones place, a 6 in the hundreds place, and a 2 in the tens place?

8 How much is ½ of ½ of ½?

9 TRUE OR FALSE? When you subtract a two-digit integer from another two-digit integer, the result is always a single-digit integer.

10 Jamir is playing ring toss and needs to correctly toss 75% of his rings to win a prize. If there are 20 rings, how many does he need to toss successfully to win?

11 Which of the following is a composite number?

a. 5   b. 9   c. 29

12 TRUE OR FALSE? An integer can be a positive or negative number.

13 If 7 is the divisor and 49 is the dividend, what is the quotient?

14 If Nick can do 28 sit-ups in 20 minutes, how many sit-ups can he do in 1 hour if he continues at that pace?

15 Saya is carrying 3 one-dollar bills, 4 quarters, and 5 pennies in her pocket. If she pulls out one of those items in her pocket at random, what is the probability she pulls out a coin?

16 The angle opposite the hypotenuse in a right triangle has how many degrees?

17 The numbers 20 and 24 have how many common factors?

18 If a triangle has sides of 5, 5, and 6, what is its area?

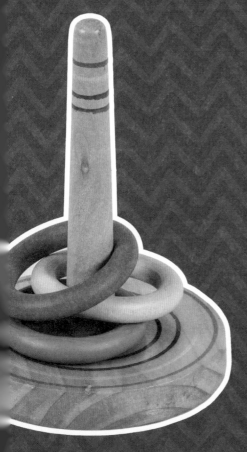

19 What is 2 to the 6th power?

20 If 6 squared is 36, then -6 squared is equal to what?

21 Multiplying what decimal by 0.1 will give you a product of 0.034?

22 If there are 2 red marbles and 3 green marbles in a bag, what's the percentage probability of pulling a red marble out of the bag?

23 What Greek letter represents the ratio of a circle's circumference to its diameter?

24 In the set of numbers 3, x, 8, and 7, if the range of the set is 7, and 3 is the lowest number, what is x?

25 How much is 4 to the 3rd power?

26 The mathematical expression (4 × 2) × 5 = 4 × (2 × 5) is an example of which property of multiplication?

    a. associative property

    b. commutative property

    c. transitive property

27 What is the only positive integer that is neither prime nor composite?

28 If you divide 30 by ½ and then add 10 to the answer, what number is the result?

29 Tristan and Amira are sharing a pizza. If the radius of the pizza is 6.2, what is the diameter?

30 Cooper's band won $35 in a contest. Each band member got $11, and there was $2 left over. How many band members are there?

31 The product of any given number and its reciprocal is always what number?

32 What number equals 10 to the 4th power?

33 A geometric pyramid with 3 faces and a base has a height of 20. If the base has an area of 30, what is the volume of that pyramid?

34 What is the additive inverse of 12?

35 By definition, "a bushel and a peck" is equivalent to how many gallons?

CURIOUS ABOUT SCIENCE

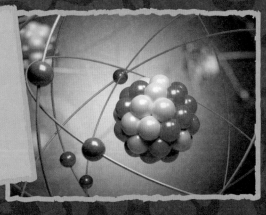

1 All other things being equal, which of the following weighs the most?

    a. a cup of ice

    b. a cup of steam

    c. a cup of liquid water

2 By definition, when water evaporates it becomes which of the following?

    a. solid

    b. gas

    c. it remains a liquid

3 TRUE OR FALSE? Electric eels are capable of giving off an electrical shock.

4 By definition, a lumen is a unit that measures which of the following?

    a. heat

    b. light

    c. sound

5 TRUE OR FALSE? A nonmagnetic piece of iron wire becomes magnetized when electricity runs through it.

6 Meaning "made by fire," what is the word for the group of rocks that includes granite and pumice?

7 TRUE OR FALSE? If an object has negative buoyancy it will float in water.

8 **TRUE OR FALSE?** Light waves and sound waves always travel at the exact same speed.

9 **TRUE OR FALSE?** When a marble rolls down a sloped plane, potential energy turns to kinetic energy.

10 Named after its French creator, what system of reading and writing for the blind consists of over 60 characters made up of raised dots?

11 **TRUE OR FALSE?** A sound wave's pitch is primarily determined by the wave's frequency.

12 At what degree Fahrenheit does liquid water begin to turn to ice at sea level?

a. 32 degrees

b. 0 degrees

c. -100 degrees

13 **TRUE OR FALSE?** Pure quartz is a mineral.

14 **TRUE OR FALSE?** A seismograph is a device that measures the intensity of an earthquake.

BONUS THE POINT AT WHICH AN OBJECT HAS NO HEAT IS DEFINED AS "ABSOLUTE ZERO" ON WHICH TEMPERATURE SCALE?

15 What is the only color of light on the visible spectrum that can pass through a blue filter?

16 When white light is passed through a prism, which color of the visible spectrum bends the most?

17 Glass is made from which of the following?

    a. clay

    b. resin

    c. sand

18 UVA and UVB are types of radiation that come from the sun. What word do the letters "UV" stand for?

19 TRUE OR FALSE? Light, heat, and sound are all forms of energy.

20 What is the softest mineral on the Mohs scale?

    a. gypsum

    b. quartz

    c. talc

BONUS A SINGLE MOLECULE OF WATER CONTAINS HOW MANY PROTONS?

21 If an atom has the same number of electrons and protons, what type of charge will it have?

    a. negative

    b. neutral

    c. positive

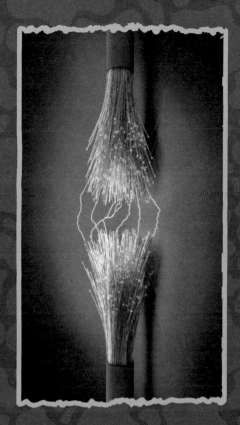

22 Which of the following is the scientific term for an organism that makes its food from inorganic materials?

    a. autotroph

    b. embryotroph

    c. heterotroph

BONUS SCIENTIST MICHAEL FARADAY COINED WHAT WORD FOR AN ATOM THAT LOSES OR GAINS AN ELECTRON AND THUS BECOMES POSITIVELY OR NEGATIVELY CHARGED?

23 A single molecule of ozone contains how many atoms of oxygen?

24 Alexander Fleming discovered what antibiotic in 1928?

BONUS MARBLE IS A METAMORPHIC ROCK FORMED FROM WHICH SEDIMENTARY ROCK?

25 The loudness of a sound is directly proportional to which of the following attributes of its sound waves?

    a. amplitude

    b. wavelength

    c. frequency

26 When referring to electricity, what word does the letter "C" stand for in the term "AC/DC"?

27 Which of the following is not considered a fossil fuel?

    a. hydrogen

    b. natural gas

    c. petroleum

28 Pressure is commonly measured in units abbreviated "psi," which stands for what four words?

29 What instrument, named in honor of the Italian scientist Luigi Galvani and invented in the 1800s, is used to measure electrical current?

BONUS ALSO KNOWN AS HYDROGEN-1, WHAT IS THE NAME FOR THE LIGHTEST AND MOST ABUNDANT ISOTOPE OF HYDROGEN?

30 An element's atomic number is determined by the quantity of what subatomic particle in its nucleus?

31 The pH scale is used to measure whether a substance is an acid or a base. What is the highest number on the pH scale?

32 Yeast belong to which kingdom of living organism?

33 TRUE OR FALSE? Atmospheric pressure is generally lower near the equator than it is near the poles.

34 In terms of size, the smallest atom belongs to what element?

35 What is the total number of atoms in two molecules of carbon dioxide?

36 What metric unit of energy is represented by the letter "J"?

37 The common abbreviation "hazmat" stands for what two words?

38 By definition, an isotope of an element is created by a variation in the number of which subatomic particle?

39 According to Newton's second law of motion, force equals mass times what third value?

40 From the Latin for "slothfulness," what physics word describes the tendency of a moving object to stay in a straight line?

41 From the Latin for "eyelash," what are the tiny hairlike projections similar to flagella that help an organism move through liquid?

42 A molecule of ammonia is made up of 3 hydrogen atoms and 1 atom of what other element?

LEARNING SHAPES

1 Which of these shapes has the fewest number of sides?
   a. rectangle
   b. square
   c. triangle

2 If Mr. Cena adds up all the sides in a triangle, a square, and a rectangle, how many sides does he have?
   a. 10
   b. 11
   c. 12

4 What is the perimeter of a regular hexagon with 5-inch sides?

3 How many total faces are there on a pair of six-sided dice?

6 Which of the following is a plane figure?
   a. cube
   b. triangle
   c. cone

5 A rectangular pyramid has a rectangular base and how many faces?

7 How many right angles does a rectangle have?

8 By definition, an octagon has how many more sides than a hexagon?

9 How many faces does a rectangular prism have?

10 Which of these is not a plane shape?
   a. cone
   b. rectangle
   c. triangle

11 Which of the following tools measures the degrees of an angle?
   a. French curve
   b. metronome
   c. protractor

12 By definition, an obtuse triangle has how many internal angles of less than 90 degrees?
   a. 1
   b. 2
   c. 3

13 A hexagon has how many more sides than a quadrilateral?

14 If we build a rectangular racetrack with sides of 20 feet and 30 feet, what is its perimeter?

15 **TRUE OR FALSE?** A single triangle can contain an acute angle, a right angle, and an obtuse angle.

16 By definition, a tangram is a puzzle consisting of how many separate flat shapes?

17 Complete the following analogy. "Pentagon" is to 5 as "heptagon" is to what number?

18 Patrick has drawn 2 isosceles triangles, 4 scalene triangles, and 6 equilateral triangles. Of these 12 triangles, how many have 2 or more sides of equal length?

19 **TRUE OR FALSE?** A regular hexagon can be divided into two trapezoids.

20 How many corners does a cube have?

22 How many pairs of parallel sides does a trapezoid have?

21 A nonagon is a shape with how many sides?

23 A trapezoid has how many pairs of opposite vertices?

24 What two-dimensional shape is formed by the intersection of a plane through the center of a sphere?

25 A rhombus contains how many interior right angles?

26 For an isosceles triangle whose interior angles are all positive integers, what is the greatest number of degrees a single interior angle can be?

27 What is the sum of the degrees of the interior angles of an octagon?

28 A polyhedron is a shape that has how many dimensions?

29 A hendecagon is a polygon with how many sides?

30 A pentagonal prism has how many total faces?

BONUS A CUBE HAS A VOLUME OF X CUBIC INCHES AND A SURFACE AREA OF X SQUARE INCHES. HOW LONG IS EACH OF ITS SIDES?

THE ELEMENTS

1. SAYA WOULD TYPICALLY USE WHICH OF THE FOLLOWING GASES TO CREATE BUBBLES IN SODA WATER?

    A. CARBON DIOXIDE B. HELIUM C. NEON

2. ON THE PERIODIC TABLE OF ELEMENTS, HYDROGEN IS CLASSIFIED AS WHICH OF THE FOLLOWING?

    A. LIQUID B. SOLID C. GAS

3. TRUE OR FALSE? ALUMINUM IS AN ELEMENT ON THE PERIODIC TABLE.

4. FIRE NEEDS THREE INGREDIENTS IN ORDER TO BURN. HEAT AND FUEL ARE TWO OF THOSE INGREDIENTS. WHAT GASEOUS ELEMENT IS THE THIRD?

5. WHAT ELEMENT IS REPRESENTED ON THE PERIODIC TABLE BY THE SYMBOL "S"?

6. IF PATRICK APPLIES ENORMOUS PRESSURE TO TWO ATOMS OF HYDROGEN, HE CAN FUSE THEM TOGETHER TO FORM WHAT NEW ELEMENT?

7. THE ATOMIC SYMBOL "Fe" STANDS FOR WHAT METAL?

BONUS THE METALLIC ELEMENT LEAD IS ON THE PERIODIC TABLE WITH WHAT TWO-LETTER SYMBOL?

8 WHAT ELEMENT, DESIGNATED "CL", EXISTS AT ROOM TEMPERATURE AS A GREENISH-YELLOW GAS?

9 WHAT METALLIC ELEMENT COMMONLY USED IN THE MAKING OF JEWELRY IS DENOTED BY THE SYMBOL "Pt"?

10 ON THE PH SCALE, WHAT DOES THE LETTER "H" REPRESENT?

11 A MOLECULE OF OZONE, THE GAS IN OUR ATMOSPHERE THAT PROTECTS US FROM UV RADIATION, IS COMPOSED ENTIRELY OF WHAT ELEMENT?

12 WHAT IS THE CHEMICAL NAME OF THE GAS THAT IS PRODUCED WHEN AMIRA MIXES BAKING SODA WITH VINEGAR?

13 IN TERMS OF WEIGHT, WHAT ELEMENT THAT EXISTS AS A SOLID AT ROOM TEMPERATURE IS THE LIGHTEST ALKALI METAL ON THE PERIODIC TABLE?

14 THE EXISTENCE OF WHAT ELEMENTAL GAS WAS DISCOVERED IN 1868 BY TWO EUROPEAN SCIENTISTS STUDYING THE SUN'S RAYS DURING A SOLAR ECLIPSE?

15 NAMED FOR A PLANET IN OUR SOLAR SYSTEM, WHAT ELEMENT HAS THE SYMBOL "U" ON THE PERIODIC TABLE?

BONUS WHAT CHEMICAL ELEMENT ON THE PERIODIC TABLE COMES LAST ALPHABETICALLY?

ALL AROUND US

MEASURING FUN!

1 How many total ½-inches are in a foot?

2 **TRUE OR FALSE?**
A toothpick 6 centimeters long is shorter than a key that is 3 inches long.

3 Which of the following is not a metric unit of measurement?
   a. pint
   b. liter
   c. gram

4 **TRUE OR FALSE?**
Lines of latitude run perpendicular to the equator.

5 If 1 inch represents 9 miles on a map, how many miles would 7 inches indicate?

6 Which of the following is equal to one acre?
   a. 4,356 square feet
   b. 43,560 square feet
   c. 435,600 square feet

7 If Cooper has 3 books that each weigh 2 pounds, 7 ounces, how many total ounces do they weigh?

8 Which of the following is the smallest in area?
   a. an acre
   b. a square mile
   c. a hectare

9 When measuring latitude, each degree can be subdivided into how many "minutes of arc"?

10 How many tablespoons are equivalent to one fluid ounce?

11 How many minutes are in one day?

12 What unit of measurement was originally created by the Romans to describe the distance covered by 1,000 paces of a soldier?

13 If your mom sends you to the store for 3 gallons of ice cream but the store only sells pints, how many pints must you buy?

14 It takes 7 gallons and 1 quart of paint to paint your house. You have 4 gallons, 3 quarts. How much more paint do you need?

15 How many watts are in a gigawatt?

16 What 18th-century Swedish scientist gave his name to a scale that measures temperature?

17 24 pints of paint is equal to how many gallons?

MONEY MATH

1 TRUE OR FALSE? FOR AS LONG AS THEY HAVE BEEN MINTED, US PENNIES HAVE BEEN 99.99 PERCENT COPPER.

2 IF COOPER IS HOLDING THE SMALLEST CURRENT US COIN IN TERMS OF CIRCUMFERENCE, WHAT COIN IS HE HOLDING?

3 TRUE OR FALSE? USING CURRENT US COINS, THE ONLY WAY TO MAKE 11 CENTS IS TO HAVE ONE DIME AND ONE PENNY.

4 IN THE US, WHAT COIN REPRESENTS EXACTLY 10 PERCENT OF A DOLLAR?
A. NICKEL   B. DIME   C. QUARTER

5 IN US CURRENCY, IF NICK HAS 437 CENTS AND CHLOE HAS 363 CENTS, AND THEY POOL THEIR MONEY, WHAT IS THE TOTAL NUMBER OF DOLLARS THEY HAVE TOGETHER?

6 MR. CENA BUYS A RULER THAT COSTS $1.26 INCLUDING TAX AND PAYS WITH A $5 BILL. WHAT'S THE TOTAL AMOUNT OF MONEY HE RECEIVES BACK?

7

IF MIA HAS A PENNY, A NICKEL, A DIME, A QUARTER, A $1 BILL, A $5 BILL, A $10 BILL, A $20 BILL, A $50 BILL, AND A $100 BILL, HOW MUCH MONEY DOES SHE HAVE?

8

WHAT IS THE LOWEST DENOMINATION OF CURRENT US PAPER CURRENCY THAT DOES NOT FEATURE THE PORTRAIT OF A US PRESIDENT ON ITS FRONT?

9

IF YOU FOUND 4 CURRENT US COINS UNDER THE COUCH CUSHION AND THEY ADDED UP TO 25 CENTS, 3 OF THE COINS MUST BE WHAT DENOMINATION?

10

THE $2 BILL FEATURES A PORTRAIT OF WHAT MAN WHO WAS THE THIRD US PRESIDENT?

11

WHAT IS THE OFFICIAL CURRENCY OF DENMARK?

BONUS IF SAYA HAS A POCKETFUL OF ZLOTYS, SHE IS CARRYING THE OFFICIAL CURRENCY OF WHAT EUROPEAN COUNTRY?

DAYS, WEEKS, AND MONTHS

1 What is the only US federal holiday that cannot fall on a Monday?

2 A day and a half is equivalent to how many hours?

3 On a US calendar, what is the maximum number of days a month can have?

4 TRUE OR FALSE? If during a given year, December 3rd falls on a Monday, then December 12th will be on a Friday.

5 On a US calendar, what is the maximum number of days a month can have?

6 TRUE OR FALSE? In the spring, when daylight saving time begins in the US, clocks turn back one hour from standard time.

7 If November 1st falls on a Monday, the US holiday of Thanksgiving is celebrated on what date?

BONUS WHICH MONTH OF OUR YEAR IS NAMED AFTER THE WIFE OF THE ROMAN GOD JUPITER?

8 In the southern hemisphere, the month of March is divided between two different seasons. Name both of them.

9 In the United States, the Memorial Day national holiday is officially observed on what day of the week?

10 A celebration of the return of spring, the European holiday of May Day is traditionally observed on what date?

11 Of the people who have US federal holidays named after them, who was the only one born in Italy?

12 In a leap year, the 365th day of the year falls on what date?

13 How many odd-numbered days are in the month of February during a non-leap year?

14 What month is named for the Roman god of war?

15 In what month did the Pilgrims on the *Mayflower* land in North America?

16 Mr. Cena went on vacation and was gone for exactly one week. What is the total number of hours he was away?

TALK ABOUT TIME!

1. IF THE CLOCK IS SET AT 8:00 A.M. AND THE TEACHER MOVES THE HOUR HAND 3 HOURS CLOCKWISE, WHAT TIME DOES IT READ NOW?

2. IF A STANDARD CLOCK READS 5:35 P.M., THE MINUTE HAND IS POINTING TO WHAT NUMBER?

3. IF IT IS 4:37 P.M. ON A STANDARD CLOCK, HOW MANY TOTAL MINUTES WILL PASS UNTIL THE NEXT TIME THE MINUTE HAND IS EXACTLY ON THE 6?

4. IF SAYA AND HER FRIENDS PLAY UNO FROM EXACTLY 6:15 P.M. TO 7:00 P.M. EVERY NIGHT, HOW MUCH TIME DO THEY SPEND AT THE POKER TABLE IN ONE WEEK?

5. IF IT IS 10:00 A.M. IN SALT LAKE CITY, UTAH, WHAT TIME IS IT IN CLEVELAND, OHIO?

6. A SESQUICENTENNIAL IS AN ANNIVERSARY THAT MARKS THE PASSAGE OF HOW MANY YEARS?

LET'S TALK SPORTS

1 Quinne has 176 baseball cards and buys 35 more. Amira has 72 baseball cards and buys 149 more. Who now has more baseball cards in total?

2 What noun is the object in the following sentence? "Saya threw the ball."

3 If a class of 16 students splits evenly into 2 separate teams for a game of dodgeball at recess, how many total students are there per team?

4 Chloe shot 5 arrows in archery class. If 3 arrows hit the 20-point circle and 2 arrows hit the 50-point bull's-eye, how many points did Chloe score?

5 If Mia's tetherball rope is 10 feet long and she swings it so 36 inches of rope wrap around the pole, how many feet of rope are free?

6 If Isabella is playing the sport invented in December 1891 by James Naismith, which sport is she playing?

7 In what geological era did football develop?
a. Cenozoic
b. Mesozoic
c. Paleozoic

8 If LeBron James scored 400 points over the course of 10 NBA regulation games, how many points did he average per quarter?

CARS, TRAINS, SHIPS, AND PLANES

1 What part of speech is the word "green" in the following sentence? "Jack wants to buy a green car when he gets his license."

    a. verb

    b. adverb

    c. adjective

2 If Colin wants to become an aviator when he grows up, he would, by definition, operate which of the following?

    a. plane

    b. train

    c. boat

3 If Mr. Cena were on a submarine, which of the following would he most likely use to help navigate?

    a. microscope

    b. periscope

    c. telescope

4 Officially known as the Space Transportation System, the space shuttle program is overseen by what US government agency?

5 What 19th-century mail service in the US carried letters over 2,000 miles in 10 days by horseback?

6 Because of efficiency from assembly-line production, the price of the Model T car was lowered from $850 in 1908 to less than $300 in 1925. What man founded the company that made it?

9 Tom can make 3 model airplanes in 4 hours. At that rate, how long will it take him to make 5 model airplanes?

10 In which century was the first automobile invented?

 a. 18th century

 b. 19th century

 c. 20th century

7 First launched in 1900, what mode of transportation, named for its German inventor, featured a large chamber with a metal skeleton that was filled with hydrogen?

8 The USSR successfully launched the first artificial satellite into space, called Sputnik 1. In what year was it launched?

11 If Quinne travels in a high-speed train moving at 520 miles an hour for 3½ hours, how many miles has she traveled?

12 If a car is traveling 120 miles per hour, how many feet per minute is it traveling?

FOOD & DRINK

1 IF AMIRA DIVIDES A PIE INTO QUARTERS AND EATS ONE SLICE, HOW MANY SLICES ARE LEFT?

2 SAYA MADE 15 BOWLS OF SPAGHETTI. IF MIA AND COLIN EAT 2 BOWLS EACH, HOW MANY BOWLS DOES SAYA HAVE LEFT?

3 IN TERMS OF VOLUME, WHICH OF THE FOLLOWING IS THE LARGEST?

    A. CUP OF JUICE   B. PINT OF JUICE   C. QUART OF JUICE

4 **TRUE OR FALSE?** SUGARS ARE CARBOHYDRATES.

5 JAMIR CAN BAKE 20 LOAVES OF BREAD IN 4 HOURS. AT THAT RATE, HOW MANY LOAVES WILL HE BAKE IN 7 HOURS?

6 IF MIA HAS A POUND AND A HALF OF POPCORN AND SHE'S PUTTING IT INTO 1-OUNCE BOWLS, WHAT IS THE TOTAL NUMBER OF BOWLS SHE NEEDS TO FILL IN ORDER TO USE ALL THE POPCORN?

7 HOW MANY TOTAL CUPS OF LEMONADE DOES CHLOE NEED TO COMPLETELY FILL A PITCHER THAT HAS A VOLUME OF A QUART AND A HALF?

THE GREAT OUTDOORS

EXPLORE THE OCEAN

1 WHAT OCEAN COVERS A THIRD OF THE SURFACE OF THE EARTH ALL BY ITSELF?

2 WHAT IS THE ONLY OCEAN NAMED FOR A COUNTRY?

3 TRUE OR FALSE? THE CONTINENT OF SOUTH AMERICA BORDERS THE PACIFIC OCEAN.

4 IN TERMS OF AREA, WHAT IS THE LARGEST OCEAN THAT BORDERS THE UNITED STATES?

5 BRAZIL HAS OVER 4,500 MILES OF COASTLINE ALONG WHICH OCEAN?

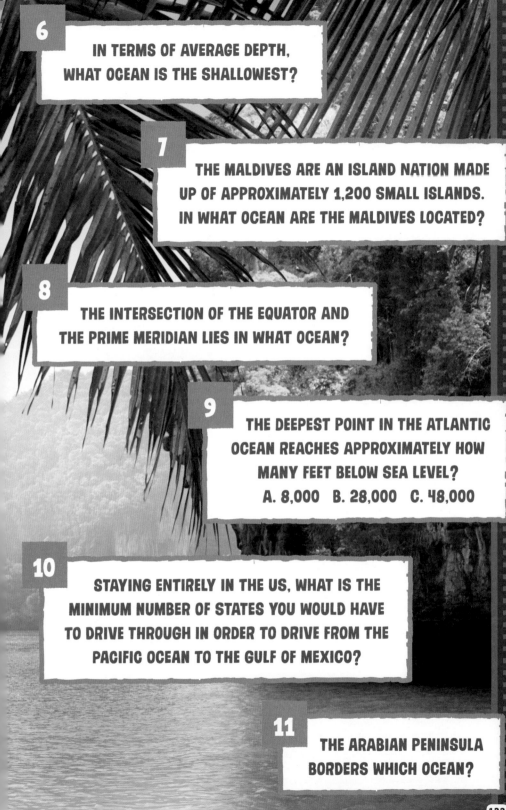

6 IN TERMS OF AVERAGE DEPTH, WHAT OCEAN IS THE SHALLOWEST?

7 THE MALDIVES ARE AN ISLAND NATION MADE UP OF APPROXIMATELY 1,200 SMALL ISLANDS. IN WHAT OCEAN ARE THE MALDIVES LOCATED?

8 THE INTERSECTION OF THE EQUATOR AND THE PRIME MERIDIAN LIES IN WHAT OCEAN?

9 THE DEEPEST POINT IN THE ATLANTIC OCEAN REACHES APPROXIMATELY HOW MANY FEET BELOW SEA LEVEL?
A. 8,000   B. 28,000   C. 48,000

10 STAYING ENTIRELY IN THE US, WHAT IS THE MINIMUM NUMBER OF STATES YOU WOULD HAVE TO DRIVE THROUGH IN ORDER TO DRIVE FROM THE PACIFIC OCEAN TO THE GULF OF MEXICO?

11 THE ARABIAN PENINSULA BORDERS WHICH OCEAN?

WILD WEATHER

1

TRUE OR FALSE? The sun is always in front of you when you see a rainbow.

2

TRUE OR FALSE? When the weather is humid, the air is holding more water vapor than when it's not humid.

3

TRUE OR FALSE? Each color of the rainbow has its own wavelength.

4

Which of the following clouds are between 0 and 6,500 feet from the surface of the earth?
a. nimbostratus
b. cirrus
c. altocumulus

5

In 1971, Theodore Fujita developed the Fujita scale to measure the damage caused by what natural phenomenon?
- a. tornadoes
- b. earthquakes
- c. hurricanes

6

Recorded in Death Valley, California, the highest temperature in US history was which of the following?
- a. 134 degrees Fahrenheit
- b. 154 degrees Fahrenheit
- c. 174 degrees Fahrenheit

7

TRUE OR FALSE?
Tornadoes can generate wind speeds as high as 300 miles per hour.

8

Which of the following clouds form farthest from the surface of the earth?
- a. cirrus
- b. nimbostratus
- c. stratocumulus

BONUS THE SPIRAL SHAPE OF A HURRICANE IS THE RESULT OF WHAT COUNTERCLOCKWISE MOVEMENT IN THE NORTHERN HEMISPHERE NAMED FOR A FRENCH PHYSICIST?

MOUNTAINS OF THE WORLD

1. If Nick plans on visiting the three tallest mountains in the world, what continent will he be visiting?

2. Mountains, valleys, and rivers occupy what layer of the earth?

   a. core

   b. crust

   c. mantle

3. The Rocky Mountains are located on what continent?

4. What state would you visit to see Rocky Mountain National Park?

5. Mount Olympus, which is over 9,000 feet tall, is the highest mountain in what country?

6. The Himalaya mountains started to form approximately how many years ago?

   a. 5 million

   b. 50 million

   c. 500 million

7. Aconcagua is the highest mountain on what continent?

8. "House of snow" is the literal translation of the name of which Asian mountain range that is home to several of the tallest mountains on earth?

9. Over 14,000 feet high, Mount Rainier is a volcanic mountain peak in what US state?

10 What mountain range in South America is the source of the Amazon River?

11 The Ural Mountains are primarily located in what country?

12 At 16,050 feet above sea level, Vinson Massif is the highest mountain on what continent?

13 The highest peaks of the Ozark Mountains are in what US state?

14 If Tristan is on Mount Fuji, he is on the tallest mountain in what country?

15 The Atlas Mountains are located on what continent?

    a. Africa

    b. Asia

    c. Europe

16 The Deccan Plateau and the Eastern Ghats mountain range are located in what country?

17 The majority of the Ozark Mountains lie in what US state?

18 The Black Forest is a wooded mountain range in the southwest of what European country?

19 If Quinne is standing on the tallest mountain in the Alps, what mountain is she standing on?

20 What mountain range includes Mount Rainier and Mount St. Helens?

21 Located in northeastern Tanzania, what is the highest mountain in Africa?

RAGING RIVERS

1. If Amira goes sailing on the longest river in the world, what river is she sailing on?

2. What river forms the border between the states of Arkansas and Mississippi?

3. If Mia is visiting the last US state the Mississippi River flows through before reaching the Gulf of Mexico, what state is she in?

4. What is the last country the Colorado River flows through before it reaches the Gulf of California?

5. **TRUE OR FALSE?** The Mississippi River primarily flows from east to west.

6. The Wabash River begins in Ohio and passes through which other state before it reaches Illinois?

7. Which of these rivers lies entirely within the US?

   a. Colorado River

   b. Mississippi River

   c. Yukon River

8. What American river, which is over 2,300 miles long, forms the border between the states of Nebraska and Iowa?

9 The Schuylkill River flows through the city of Philadelphia, Pennsylvania, and then empties into what other river?

10 The Red River of the North is over 900 miles long and is located on the border between North Dakota and what other US state?

11 The River Shannon is over 240 miles long, making it the longest river in what European country?

12 What river forms the border between New Jersey and Pennsylvania?

13 Alexandria, Virginia, is located along the banks of what river that is over 350 miles long?

14 The Murray-Darling is the longest river system in what country?

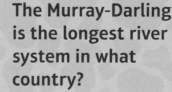

15 The Salmon River is the largest tributary of the Snake River. In what US state is it located?

16 With a length of over 3,900 miles, what is the longest river in Asia?

17 The Volga is the longest river in Europe. What is the second-longest river on the continent?

18 If you're traveling down the Zambezi River in Africa, you'll come to what waterfall that was named after a British monarch by explorer David Livingstone?

19 Two rivers flow through our nation's capital, Washington, DC. The Potomac is one of them; what is the other?

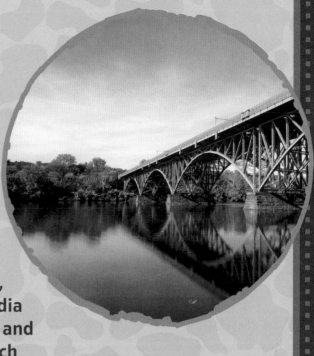

20 The Ganges River originates in the Himalayas, flows through India and Bangladesh, and empties into which bay that is part of the Indian Ocean?

21 Name this river that connects the Great Lakes to the Atlantic Ocean.

22 What is the name of the longest river in Canada, which is named for the explorer who discovered it in 1789?

23 What river forms the boundary between the US states of South Carolina and Georgia?

24 Hudson Bay and the Hudson River are named for an English explorer who had what first name?

25 The Yukon River flows through what US state?

ERUPTING VOLCANOES!

1 TRUE OR FALSE? SOME VOLCANOES ARE UNDERWATER.

2 TRUE OR FALSE? PUMICE IS FORMED FROM THE LAVA OF VOLCANOES.

3 FORMED FROM LAVA, OBSIDIAN IS WHICH OF THE FOLLOWING TYPES OF ROCK?

A. IGNEOUS   B. METAMORPHIC   C. SEDIMENTARY

4 WHAT DORMANT VOLCANO, WHICH IS OVER 13,000 FEET TALL, IS THE TALLEST MOUNTAIN IN HAWAII?

5 THE MOUNT PINATUBO VOLCANO IS LOCATED ON WHAT SOUTHEAST ASIAN ISLAND COUNTRY?

6 WHICH OF THE FOLLOWING IS A TYPE OF VOLCANO?

A. GORGE   B. NIMBUS   C. SHIELD

7 THE LARGEST VOLCANO IN OUR SOLAR SYSTEM, OLYMPUS MONS IS LOCATED ON WHAT PLANET?

8 IN AD 79, THE CITIES OF HERCULANEUM AND POMPEII WERE BURIED AS A RESULT OF THE ERUPTION OF WHICH VOLCANO?

9 THE ACTIVE VOLCANO MOUNT ETNA IS THE HIGHEST MOUNTAIN ON WHAT MEDITERRANEAN ISLAND?

LAKE WONDERS

1 TRUE OR FALSE? By definition, all lakes are composed solely of fresh water.

2 Two countries border the Great Lakes. The United States is one of them. What is the other?

3 Which of the following is the name of one of the Great Lakes?
a. Lake Huron
b. Lake Quebec
c. Lake Winnipeg

4 The Salton Sea is a lake located in what US state?

5 Michigan, Minnesota, and Wisconsin all border what Great Lake?

6 What is the only US state to border Lake Ontario?

7 The St. Lawrence River flows out of what Great Lake?

8 Which of the Great Lakes comes first alphabetically?

9 Lake Michigan borders how many US states?

10 Together, the Great Lakes border a total of how many US states?

11 The Erie Canal connects the Great Lakes to what New York river?

BONUS LOCATED IN RUSSIA, WHAT IS THE NAME OF THE OLDEST, DEEPEST FRESHWATER LAKE IN THE WORLD?

PARKS ROAD TRIP

1 The geyser Old Faithful erupts on average every 90 minutes in what US national park?

2 **TRUE OR FALSE?** The tallest tree in the world is an evergreen.

3 What US national park has the greatest number of geysers?

4 Of the following biomes, which one covers the greatest amount of Earth's land area?

    a. arctic tundra

    b. deserts

    c. forests

5 If Jamir goes hiking in Haleakala National Park, what Hawaiian island is he on?

6 If Saya is visiting Great Basin National Park, home to the historic Lehman Caves, then she is in what US state?

7 Which of the following would be an example of a biome?

    a. human heartbeat

    b. stalk of broccoli

    c. tropical rainforest

8 With redwood trees over 240 feet tall, Muir Woods National Monument is located in what US state?

9 Minute Man National Historical Park, which commemorates the opening battle in the American Revolution, is located in what US state?

10 Known as the "Father of the National Parks," what American naturalist founded and became the first president of the Sierra Club in 1892?

11 The word "jungle" comes from the word "jangal," which means "impenetrable forest" in what language?

a. French

b. Hindi

c. Spanish

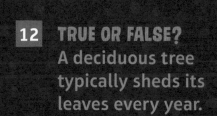

12 TRUE OR FALSE? A deciduous tree typically sheds its leaves every year.

BONUS WHAT US STATE IS HOME TO HOT SPRINGS NATIONAL PARK?

13 Home to the world's longest cave system, Mammoth Cave National Park is located in what US state?

SEE THE SEAS

1   THE NETHERLANDS BORDERS WHICH OF THE
    FOLLOWING SEAS?

         A. ARAL SEA   B. MEDITERRANEAN SEA
                  C. NORTH SEA

2   THE DEAD SEA IS THE LOWEST POINT
    OF ELEVATION ON WHAT
    CONTINENT?

3   THE ISLAND OF CORFU IN THE
    MEDITERRANEAN SEA IS PART
    OF WHAT COUNTRY?

4   BAKU, THE CAPITAL OF THE COUNTRY OF AZERBAIJAN,
    IS LOCATED ON THE SHORE OF WHICH SEA?

5   THE TYRRHENIAN SEA IS BORDERED ON THE EAST BY
    WHAT EUROPEAN COUNTRY?

6   THE SUEZ CANAL, COMPLETED IN THE 1800S,
    CONNECTS THE MEDITERRANEAN SEA WITH WHAT
    OTHER SEA?

7 THE COUNTRY OF TURKEY IS BORDERED ON THE NORTH BY WHAT SEA?

8 IF YOU ARE STANDING ON THE SHORE OF THE BALTIC SEA, WHAT CONTINENT ARE YOU ON?

9 THE ISLANDS OF CYPRUS AND MAJORCA ARE LOCATED IN WHAT SEA?

10 PART OF THE MEDITERRANEAN, WHAT SMALLER SEA IS LOCATED BETWEEN GREECE AND ASIA MINOR?

11 IN TERMS OF LAND AREA, WHAT IS THE LARGEST ISLAND IN THE MEDITERRANEAN SEA?

PLANT LIFE

1 **TRUE OR FALSE?** The red maple tree is deciduous and may shed its leaves in winter.

2 The carrots you typically eat come from what part of the carrot plant?

    a. flower

    b. root

    c. stalk

3 Which of the following does a seed typically grow first?

    a. flower

    b. leaves

    c. roots

4 What US holiday officially founded by J. Sterling Morton celebrates the planting of trees?

BONUS LYING BETWEEN THE BARK AND THE WOOD, WHAT IS THE WORD FOR THE CELLULAR LAYER FOUND IN WOODY PLANTS THAT SEPARATES THE XYLEM FROM THE PHLOEM?

5 **TRUE OR FALSE?** Wheat and barley are edible grasses.

6 Which of the following fruits typically has more than one seed per fruit?

    a. cherry

    b. apple

    c. peach

7 **TRUE OR FALSE?** Some species of grass have flowers.

8 **TRUE OR FALSE?** In a peapod, the peas are seeds.

9 Which of the following plants have aerial roots?

    a. orchids

    b. palm trees

    c. sunflowers

10 Which of the following plants is an example of a succulent?

    a. Douglas fir

    b. saguaro cactus

    c. sunflower

11 The vanilla bean is harvested from which of the following types of plants?

    a. palm tree

    b. orchid

    c. water lily

12 Which of the following is a female part of a flower?

    a. anther

    b. ovule

    c. stamen

13 TRUE OR FALSE? Mushrooms typically use photosynthesis to produce food.

14 Which of the following is the oldest part of a tree?

    a. bark

    b. heartwood

    c. sapwood

15 TRUE OR FALSE? Bamboo is a species of grass.

16 TRUE OR FALSE? Moss is an example of a nonvascular plant.

17 During photosynthesis, what gas do plants take in and combine with water to form glucose?

18 Plants take in carbon dioxide through tiny holes on the bottom of their leaves called which of the following?

    a. chlorophyll

    b. phloem

    c. stomata

19 Lima beans, lentils, and peas are all members of what family of plants?

20 Tropical rainforests have four basic layers of trees. Which of these is not a layer in a tropical rainforest?

    a. canopy

    b. nimbus

    c. understory

21 Located in California, the oldest living tree in the United States is a member of what species?

22 What color in the visible light spectrum does chlorophyll in plants absorb the least?

23 Also known as tocopherol, what vitamin is found in avocado, peanuts, and sunflower seeds?

PEOPLE & PLACES

AROUND THE GLOBE

1 Christopher Columbus's voyages to America were funded by the king and queen of what country?

2 If Quinne is visiting the nation of Thailand, what continent is she on?

3 How many of the seven continents have two-word names?

4 What country has red-coated policemen who are nicknamed "Mounties"?

5 In terms of land area, which of the seven continents is the second smallest?

6 Excluding Greenland, what is the third-largest country in North America in terms of area?

7 The pyramids of Giza are located in what modern-day country?

8 If Colin kayaks to the only continent with no countries, what continent is the conclusion of Colin's kayaking quest?

9 Which of the seven continents was the last to be discovered?

10 The Gulf of Aden separates Africa from what other continent?

11 Reykjavík is the capital of what island country?

BONUS IN 1804, AN ARMY COMPOSED PRIMARILY OF FORMER SLAVES DEFEATED THEIR COLONIAL MASTERS TO FORM WHAT MODERN CARIBBEAN COUNTRY?

12 In what century was the religion of Islam founded?

   a. 7th century BC

   b. 7th century AD

   c. 14th century AD

13 The kimono is a type of robe that originated and was popularized in what country?

14 The jet stream that blows across the continental United States generally moves in what cardinal direction?

16 Which of the following Mediterranean islands extends the farthest south?

  a. Corsica

  b. Sardinia

  c. Sicily

15 Which of the following is the highest level in a tropical rainforest?

  a. canopy layer

  b. understory layer

  c. emergent layer

BONUS WHAT RIVER FLOWS THROUGH THE CAPITAL CITIES OF BOTH CAMBODIA AND LAOS?

17 Approximately what percentage of Earth's human population lives in the northern hemisphere?

  a. 30 percent

  b. 60 percent

  c. 90 percent

18 TRUE OR FALSE? The island of Barbados is an independent country.

19 Which one of Japan's main islands is the largest in area?

20 The Forbidden City in Beijing, China, was built during the reign of what dynasty that ruled from 1368 to 1644?

21 What European country is a volcanic island located on the Mid-Atlantic Ridge?

22 The nation of Guyana lies on what continent?

23 Which of the following continents has the greatest human population?

    a. Europe

    b. North America

    c. South America

24 Over 250,000 square miles in area, the Patagonian Desert is located on what continent?

25 Kuala Lumpur is the capital of what Asian country?

BONUS THE INTERNATIONAL MERIDIAN CONFERENCE IN 1884 DESIGNATED THAT THE PRIME MERIDIAN PASS THROUGH AN OBSERVATORY IN WHICH BOROUGH OF LONDON, ENGLAND?

26 In 1871, a group of independent states, including Bavaria and Prussia, unified to create what modern-day European country?

27 Which of the following historical leaders was born first?

    a. Alexander the Great

    b. Julius Caesar

    c. William the Conqueror

28 The Sinai Peninsula connects Asia to what other continent?

29 Transylvania is a mountainous region located in what European country?

30 What bridge, completed in 1964, is the longest suspension bridge in North America?

31 In 1898, what country leased Hong Kong from China for 99 years?

32 Moscow became the capital of Russia in 1918. What city was the capital immediately before that?

BONUS WHAT IS THE NAME OF THE BAY THAT BORDERS INDIA TO THE EAST?

33 In terms of area, what is the largest island in the Caribbean?

34 The US state of Maine has land borders with New Brunswick and what other Canadian province?

35 "Shogun" was the title given to the military men who were the primary leaders of what country during the years 1192 to 1867?

36 In 1789, an angry mob set off a revolution by storming a prison called the Bastille in what city?

37 The Galápagos Islands are part of what country?

38 What is the capital of Turkey?

39 The signing of the Treaty of Córdoba in 1821 gave what modern-day country its independence from Spain?

40 The Berlin Wall once separated East Berlin from West Berlin. Construction of the wall began in what decade?

BONUS KNOWN FOR THE NARWHAL POPULATION ALONG ITS COAST, BAFFIN ISLAND BELONGS TO WHAT COUNTRY?

45 Buenos Aires is the capital and largest city of what South American country?

BONUS IN WHAT YEAR DID THE BRITISH PASSENGER SHIP *TITANIC* SINK ON ITS MAIDEN VOYAGE ACROSS THE ATLANTIC?

46 Built by the Moors over 600 years ago, the Alhambra is a palace located in what modern-day country?

47 During World War I, what British luxury ocean liner was torpedoed and sunk by a German submarine on May 7, 1915?

41 The ancient civilization of Mycenae was located in what modern-day country?

42 If Chloe is on the island of Luzon, she is visiting the largest island of what country?

48 The country of Bangladesh in Asia is home to over 150 million people. It has land borders with India and what other country?

BONUS THE ISLAND OF ZANZIBAR IS A PART OF WHAT AFRICAN COUNTRY?

43 Before the revolution of 1917, the Romanovs were the monarchs of what country?

49 Like the US, the country of Mexico is composed of one federal district and several different states. The US has fifty states. How many does Mexico have?

44 The Bantu group of languages are spoken primarily on which continent?

50 The Mariana Islands are a chain of volcanic islands in the western Pacific Ocean. In terms of area, what is the largest of these islands?

51 What Middle Eastern capital is the oldest continuously inhabited capital city in the world?

52 Since the late 15th century, guards from what country have been responsible for the safety of the pope in Vatican City?

BONUS WHAT IS THE ONLY COUNTRY IN THE WORLD WHOSE OFFICIAL NATIONAL FLAG IS NOT A QUADRILATERAL?

53 In the 1494 Treaty of Tordesillas, the pope divided the world between Spain and what other country?

54 In 1955, what organization of communist nations was founded in response to NATO?

55 Bordered by Russia and Azerbaijan, what is the largest inland body of water in the world in terms of surface area?

56 The United Kingdom consists of four countries. England, Northern Ireland, and Scotland are three. What is the fourth?

57 What was the original name of the city that was renamed Constantinople in the 4th century AD by Constantine the Great?

58 In 1900, the uprising known as the Boxer Rebellion attempted to drive foreigners out of what country?

59 Famed conqueror Napoleon Bonaparte was born on what island?

BONUS TWO OF THE WONDERS OF THE ANCIENT WORLD WERE LOCATED IN EGYPT. ONE WAS THE PYRAMIDS OF GIZA. WHAT WAS THE OTHER?

HISTORICAL FIGURES

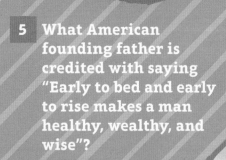

1 Famous for patenting 1,093 inventions, what American inventor was known as the Wizard of Menlo Park?

2 What inventor received the first patent for the telephone in 1876 at the age of 29?

BONUS THE WRIGHT BROTHERS WERE CREDITED WITH INVENTING THE AIRPLANE, BUT WHAT RUSSIAN-AMERICAN ENGINEER BORN IN 1889 ROSE TO FAME FOR DESIGNING THE HELICOPTER?

3 Which of the following machines was patented by Thomas Edison in the 1870s?

    a. sewing machine

    b. phonograph

    c. radio

4 Named for the inventor who created it in the 1830s, what code breaks down the alphabet into dots and dashes for sending messages?

5 What American founding father is credited with saying "Early to bed and early to rise makes a man healthy, wealthy, and wise"?

6 In 1927, what pilot made the first nonstop solo flight across the Atlantic from New York to Paris in a plane named the *Spirit of St. Louis*?

BONUS WHAT WERE THE FIRST AND LAST NAMES OF THE US COMMODORE WHO NEGOTIATED A TRADE TREATY WITH JAPAN IN 1854, ENDING HUNDREDS OF YEARS OF JAPANESE ISOLATION?

7 Born in 1822, what French chemist, known for his work in preventing bacteria in milk, also pioneered a vaccine for rabies?

8 What is the three-word radio call sign used by any U.S air force aircraft that carries the U.S president?

BONUS IN THE FAMOUS EQUATION BY ALBERT EINSTEIN E = MC², WHAT DOES THE LETTER "C" REPRESENT?

9 What electrical engineer born in 1856 in present-day Croatia helped develop alternating current electricity and also has a measurement of magnetism named after him?

10 Which British soldier and statesman led his troops to victory over Napoleon at the Battle of Waterloo and went on to become prime minister?

BONUS THE *GOLDEN HIND* WAS THE FLAGSHIP OF WHAT NAVIGATOR AND EXPLORER WHO WAS THE FIRST ENGLISHMAN TO CIRCUMNAVIGATE THE GLOBE?

11 What conquistador led the first Spanish expedition to meet with the Aztecs?

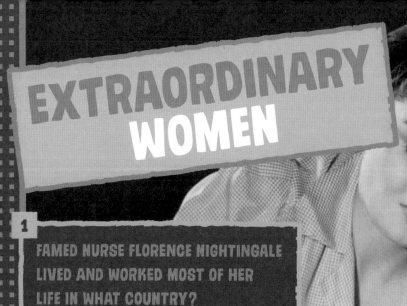

EXTRAORDINARY
WOMEN

1

FAMED NURSE FLORENCE NIGHTINGALE LIVED AND WORKED MOST OF HER LIFE IN WHAT COUNTRY?

2

IN 1979, WHO BECAME THE FIRST WOMAN TO BE FEATURED ON US CURRENCY?

3

IN WHAT YEAR DID SANDRA DAY O'CONNOR BECOME THE FIRST FEMALE US SUPREME COURT JUSTICE?

4

MARIE CURIE IS THE ONLY WOMAN TO RECEIVE A NOBEL PRIZE IN TWO DIFFERENT FIELDS. CHEMISTRY WAS ONE OF THE FIELDS; WHAT WAS THE OTHER?

5

BORN IN 1820, WHAT BRITISH NURSE WAS NICKNAMED "THE LADY WITH THE LAMP" BECAUSE SHE OFTEN WORKED THROUGH THE NIGHT TO BRING AID TO WOUNDED SOLDIERS?

6 GOLDA MEIR BECAME THE FIRST FEMALE PRIME MINISTER OF WHAT COUNTRY IN 1969?

7 WHAT NAME DID ABOLITIONIST ISABELLA BAUMFREE TAKE WHEN SHE BECAME A TRAVELING PREACHER AND DELIVERED THE SPEECH "AIN'T I A WOMAN"?

8 NOMINATED IN 1872 BY THE EQUAL RIGHTS PARTY, WHO BECAME THE FIRST WOMAN TO RUN FOR THE OFFICE OF PRESIDENT OF THE UNITED STATES, LOSING TO ULYSSES GRANT?

9 BORN IN 1866, WHAT INNOVATIVE TEACHER FOR THE BLIND AND DEAF HAD HELEN KELLER AS ONE OF HER STUDENTS?

10 IN 1955, WHO FAMOUSLY FOUGHT FOR CIVIL RIGHTS BY REFUSING TO GIVE UP HER SEAT ON AN ALABAMA BUS?

11 CLARA BARTON, A PIONEERING NURSE AND TEACHER, HELPED ORGANIZE AND BECAME THE FIRST PRESIDENT OF THIS ORGANIZATION IN 1881.

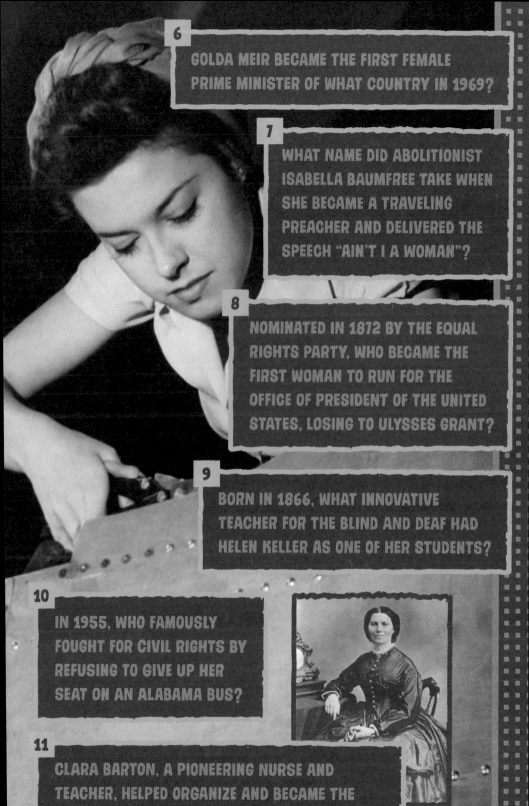

INTO THE UNKNOWN

1 In what year did Christopher Columbus embark on his first voyage to the Americas?

2 Lewis and Clark's famous 1804 expedition ended on the shores of which ocean?

3 What is the total number of ships that Christopher Columbus set sail with on his first voyage to the New World in 1492?

4 Jacques Cousteau was a Frenchman best known for exploring which of the following?
a. the deep sea
b. African deserts
c. the French Alps

5 The explorer Magellan was famous for leading the first expedition to circle the globe. What was his first name?

BONUS IN 1488, WHAT PORTUGUESE EXPLORER LED THE FIRST EUROPEAN EXPEDITION TO ROUND AFRICA'S CAPE OF GOOD HOPE?

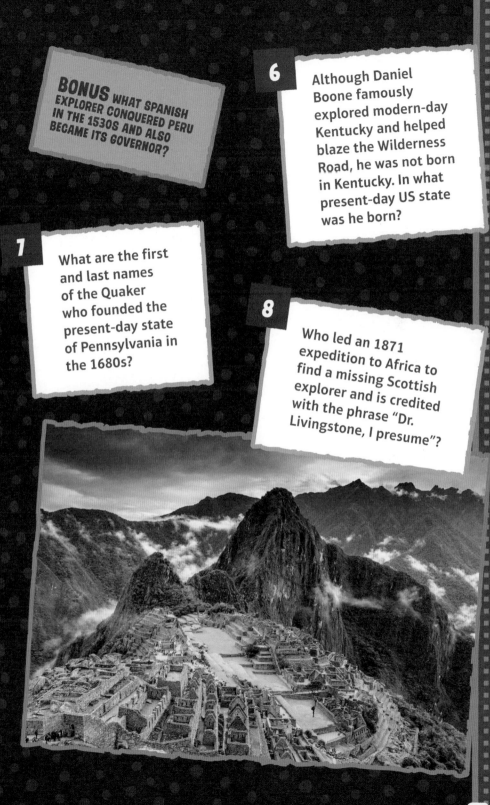

BONUS WHAT SPANISH EXPLORER CONQUERED PERU IN THE 1530S AND ALSO BECAME ITS GOVERNOR?

6 Although Daniel Boone famously explored modern-day Kentucky and helped blaze the Wilderness Road, he was not born in Kentucky. In what present-day US state was he born?

7 What are the first and last names of the Quaker who founded the present-day state of Pennsylvania in the 1680s?

8 Who led an 1871 expedition to Africa to find a missing Scottish explorer and is credited with the phrase "Dr. Livingstone, I presume"?

9 In 1911, explorer Roald Amundsen became the first person to reach the South Pole. He was from what country?

10 In 1908 and 1909, explorer Robert Peary famously led an expedition to what destination?
a. the North Pole
b. the South Pole
c. the top of Mount Everest

11 In the 13th century, Marco Polo traveled from Italy to the court of Kublai Khan in what modern-day country?

12 Sacagawea, who helped guide the Lewis and Clark expedition of the early 1800s, was a member of what Native American tribe?

13 What Spanish explorer is credited as being the first European to discover the Mississippi River, which he did in the 1540s?

BONUS WHILE LEADING A SEARCH FOR THE SEVEN GOLDEN CITIES, WHICH SPANISH CONQUISTADOR BECAME THE FIRST EUROPEAN TO EXPLORE PRESENT-DAY NEW MEXICO AND ARIZONA?

14 In the 1600s, what French explorer traveled up the St. Lawrence River and established a trading post that later became the city of Quebec, Canada?

BONUS WHAT 16TH-CENTURY GERMAN ASTRONOMER DISCOVERED THE LAW OF PLANETARY MOTION THAT STATES THAT PLANETS MOVE IN ELLIPTICAL ORBITS WITH THE SUN AT ONE FOCUS?

15 Helping to establish the spice trade, Vasco da Gama's expedition around the Cape of Good Hope eventually reached what country in May 1498?

16 The French explorer Antoine de la Mothe Cadillac founded which major US city in 1701?

BONUS ON AUGUST 3, 1492, CHRISTOPHER COLUMBUS'S FIRST VOYAGE TO THE AMERICAS DEPARTED FROM WHAT SPANISH PORT?

KINGS, QUEENS, AND RULERS

1 At its height, Alexander the Great's empire included land on how many different continents?

2 What is the name and number of the king of England who was the first Tudor monarch?

3 What Asian warrior and ruler of the Mongols led his army in an invasion of China in 1211?

4 Alexander the Great was crowned king of what ancient empire in 336 BC?

5 Although he became king of England, William the Conqueror was born in what modern-day country?

6 North and South Carolina are named for what king of England?

7 What US state was named for Queen Henrietta Maria, the wife of King Charles I of England?

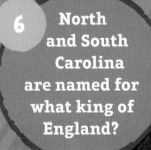

8 In Sir Thomas Malory's books about legendary King Arthur and the Knights of the Round Table, what was the name of King Arthur's queen?

BONUS WHO WAS THE LAST HAPSBURG EMPEROR OF THE AUSTRO-HUNGARIAN EMPIRE?

9 What was the name and number of the king of England during the American Revolutionary War?

BONUS WHO WAS THE KING OF ENGLAND WHEN THE MAGNA CARTA WAS ADOPTED IN 1215?

10 What general served as the prime minister of Japan during the majority of World War II?

11 What man, who ruled the Huns from AD 434 to 453, is famous for attacking large parts of the Roman Empire?

12 What ruler of the Soviet Union served as secretary general of the Communist Party from 1922 until his death in 1953?

13 What Egyptian queen gave birth to Julius Caesar's son in 47 BC?

14 What was the name of the grandfather of Ivan the Terrible who broke from the Mongols and declared himself the tsar of Russia?

BONUS WHAT KING OF SCOTLAND SUCCEEDED ELIZABETH I AS THE MONARCH OF ENGLAND?

BONUS WHAT 6TH KING OF BABYLON CREATED A CODE OF LAWS THAT INCLUDED THE CONCEPT OF "AN EYE FOR AN EYE"?

15 What was the name of the Japanese emperor who gave a speech over the radio on August 15, 1945, to announce Japan's surrender in World War II?

16 Who was queen of England when the English defeated the Spanish Armada in 1588?

17 What was the name and number of the last king of France, who was overthrown and later convicted of treason in 1792?

18 What warrior king conquered much of Europe and founded the Holy Roman Empire before he died in 814?

BONUS WHAT WAS THE NAME AND NUMBER OF THE KING WHOSE SON WAS FAMED CONQUEROR ALEXANDER THE GREAT?

ANCIENT HISTORY

1 The Roman goddess Luna was the personification of what celestial body?

2 What ancient civilization had rulers known as pharaohs?

    a. Egyptians

    b. Greeks

    c. Romans

3 The ancient Olympic Games originated during the 8th century BC in what modern-day country?

    a. Egypt

    b. Greece

    c. Italy

4 Nefertiti was a 14th-century BC queen of what ancient civilization?

5 King Tut was a ruler of what ancient civilization?

6 Which of the following ancient civilizations came first?

    a. Incas

    b. Vikings

    c. Spartans

7 The Roman numeral XXIX represents what number?

8 Which of the following was the ancient Egyptian god of the sun?

    a. Amon Ra

    b. Horus

    c. Isis

9 What Roman general became dictator for life of the Roman Republic in 44 BC, just weeks before his death?

11 During the Ice Age, North America was connected to which continent via a land bridge that now no longer exists?

12 One of the seven wonders of the ancient world, the Hanging Gardens were located in what city?

10 Greek philosopher Aristotle believed that everything was made up of four elements. Air, water, and earth were three of those elements. What was the fourth?

13 Carthage was an ancient city-state and adversary of Rome. On what continent was it located?

    a. Africa

    b. Asia

    c. Europe

14 In architecture, which type of Greek column was developed first?

    a. Corinthian

    b. Doric

    c. Ionic

18 What Greek goddess of wisdom was the equivalent of the Roman goddess Minerva?

19 The equivalent of the Roman goddess Venus, who was the Greek goddess of beauty?

15 What was the first name of the man who was emperor of Rome when approximately half the city burned in AD 64?

16 Known to the Greeks as Eros, what Roman god of love fell in love with a mortal woman named Psyche?

17 The Rosetta stone, which helped historians understand hieroglyphics, contains inscriptions in Egyptian and what other ancient language?

20 The equivalent of the Greek god Dionysus, who was the Roman god of wine, dancing, and theater?

21 The ancient Minoan civilization was founded on what island?

22 One of the seven wonders of the ancient world, the Temple of Artemis was located at Ephesus, which is now part of what country?

23 What Carthaginian leader famously marched his soldiers and elephants over the Alps to attack Roman territory in Italy?

24 The ancient region known as Mesopotamia was bordered by the Tigris and what other river?

25 What Roman general born in the 2nd century BC is credited with saying, "I came, I saw, I conquered"?

26 What ancient Athenian leader born in 490 BC initiated and oversaw construction of the Acropolis?

27 A people of Polynesian origin, the Maori are native inhabitants of what country located in the southern hemisphere?

28 Two of the seven wonders of the ancient world were located in modern-day Greece. One was the statue of Zeus at Olympia. What was the other?

BONUS KNOWN AS A NATION OF TRADERS, THE ANCIENT KINGDOM OF AKSUM WAS LOCATED ON WHAT CONTINENT?

EVERYTHING MYTHOLOGY

1 THE GREEK GODDESS GAEA WAS PRIMARILY ASSOCIATED WITH WHAT PLANET IN OUR SOLAR SYSTEM?

2 TRUE OR FALSE? THE ROMAN DEITY CERES WAS FEMALE.

3 IN GREEK MYTHOLOGY, WHAT WAS THE NAME OF THE TITAN WHO WAS GIVEN THE RESPONSIBILITY OF HOLDING UP THE HEAVENS ON HIS SHOULDERS?

4 IN GREEK MYTHOLOGY, THE GODDESS OF WISDOM, ATHENA, WAS THE DAUGHTER OF WHICH GOD?

5 IN GREEK MYTHOLOGY, WHAT WOMAN RELEASED ALL THE EVILS INTO THE WORLD AFTER LOOKING INTO A BOX SHE WAS TOLD NEVER TO OPEN?

6 IN ROMAN MYTHOLOGY, WHAT CREATURES OF THE WOODLAND WERE HALF-MAN AND HALF-GOAT?

7 IN GREEK MYTHOLOGY, WHAT PIPE-PLAYING GOD OF THE FLOCKS AND HERDS HAD THE EARS, HORNS, AND LEGS OF A GOAT?

8 WHAT FIGURE IN ROMAN MYTHOLOGY WON IMMORTALITY FOR PERFORMING 12 LABORS?

9 ACCORDING TO NORSE MYTHOLOGY, WHICH OF THE FOLLOWING GODS WAS RULER OF PEACE, SUNSHINE, AND FERTILITY?

A. FREY B. ODIN C. THOR

10 IN GREEK MYTHOLOGY, WHAT GIANT MONSTER WITH NINE HEADS, WHO LIVED IN THE MARSHES OF LERNA, WAS SLAIN BY HERCULES?

11 WHAT SYMBOL OF THE OLYMPIC GAMES COMMEMORATES THE THEFT OF FIRE FROM THE GREEK GOD ZEUS BY PROMETHEUS?

12 IN GREEK MYTHOLOGY, WHAT SON OF ZEUS SLEW MEDUSA AND HAS A CONSTELLATION NAMED IN HIS HONOR?

13 IN GREEK MYTHOLOGY, POSEIDON IS THE GOD OF THE SEA. WHAT IS THE NAME OF HIS EQUIVALENT IN ROMAN MYTHOLOGY?

14 IN GREEK MYTHOLOGY, THE GODDESS OF THE HUNT WAS NAMED ARTEMIS. WHAT IS THE NAME OF HER COUNTERPART IN ROMAN MYTHOLOGY?

15 PARALLEL TO MARS IN ROMAN MYTHOLOGY, WHAT SON OF ZEUS AND HERA WAS THE GREEK GOD OF WAR?

16 IN GREEK MYTHOLOGY, WHAT BROTHER OF ZEUS WAS THE GOD OF THE UNDERWORLD?

17 WHAT YOUTH FROM GREEK MYTHOLOGY WAS SO BEAUTIFUL HE FELL IN LOVE WITH HIS OWN REFLECTION?

18 IN GREEK MYTHOLOGY, WHAT SON OF ZEUS AND TWIN OF ARTEMIS WAS KNOWN FOR HIS GIFTS OF PROPHECY AND HEALING?

EXPLORE THE HUMAN BODY

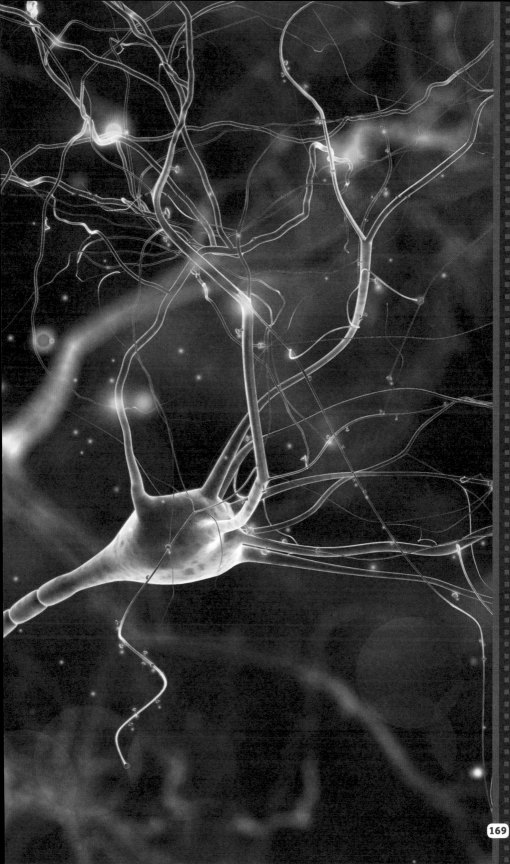

THE FANTASTIC BODY

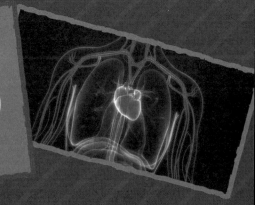

1. Quinne is a typical human; how many vocal cords does she have?

2. **TRUE OR FALSE?** The hair on the outside of your head is composed primarily of dead cells.

3. **TRUE OR FALSE?** The human elbow is a joint.

4. What word from the Latin for "hollow" describes a hole in a tooth?

5. **TRUE OR FALSE?** You use your muscles when you breathe.

6. **TRUE OR FALSE?** The tongue is an organ.

7. If Isabella wanted to view an enlarged image of an amoeba, which of the following instruments should she use?

   a. stethoscope

   b. microscope

   c. gyroscope

8. The senses of smell, touch, sight, taste, and hearing are all part of what system of the human body?

   a. circulatory

   b. digestive

   c. nervous

9. Which of the following systems moves blood throughout the human body?

   a. muscular

   b. digestive

   c. circulatory

10 The majority of blood cells in the typical human body are which of the following?

    a. red blood cells

    b. white blood cells

    c. blue blood cells

11 In the human body, which of the following is a part of the circulatory system?

    a. trachea

    b. veins

    c. spinal cord

12 TRUE OR FALSE? Strep throat is caused by bacteria.

13 TRUE OR FALSE? If you are right-handed, the nails on your right hand grow faster than those on your left.

14 The largest bone in the human body is the femur. What is the second largest?

15 Also called the voice box, what part of the human body produces vocal sounds?

16 TRUE OR FALSE? In the human body, the ribs connect to the spinal column.

17 The fibula bone is located in what part of the human body?

    a. arm

    b. leg

    c. hand

18 TRUE OR FALSE? The human thumb and forefinger have exactly the same number of bones.

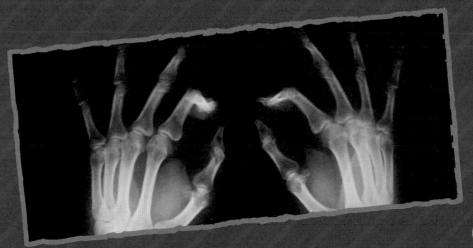

19 In the human body, which of the following regulates metabolism?

    a. immune system

    b. nervous system

    c. endocrine system

20 The phalanges are bones contained in which of the following parts of the body?

    a. ear

    b. hand

    c. jaw

21 CPR is an emergency medical procedure used when someone's heart has stopped beating. The "CP" stands for "cardiopulmonary." What word does the "R" stand for?

22 Which of the following parts of the body has the greatest number of sweat glands?

    a. back

    b. feet

    c. underarms

23 Patrick broke his clavicle in a football game. Which of these bones did he break?

    a. collarbone

    b. elbow

    c. kneecap

24 **TRUE OR FALSE?** In humans, the diaphragm is a part of the digestive system.

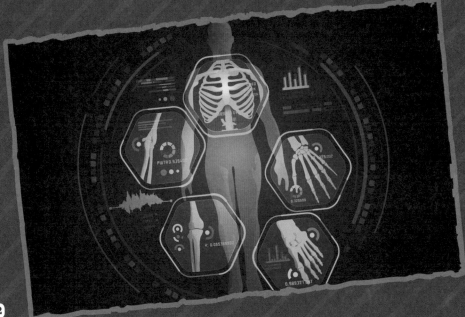

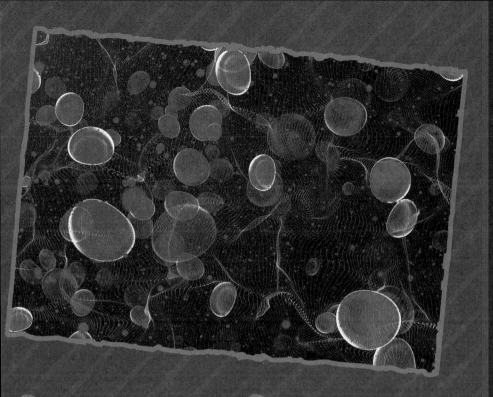

25 The average human heart pulses approximately how many times per minute?

    a. 50

    b. 90

    c. 130

26 What is the largest joint in the human body?

27 Which of the following was discovered in 1928 after a scientist found mold in a dish?

    a. insulin

    b. penicillin

    c. polio vaccine

28 The ulna is a bone located in which part of the human body?

    a. arm

    b. leg

    c. foot

29 In a full set of 32 adult human teeth, how many are molars?

30 What two-headed muscle helps bend the forearm to the upper arm?

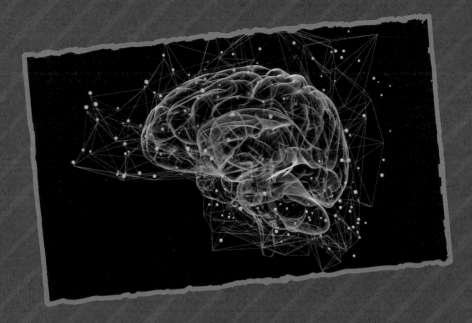

31 The human coccyx is the evolutionary remainder of which of the following body parts?

    a. gill

    b. tail

    c. wing

32 Located in the neck, what endocrine gland in the human body uses iodine to make hormones?

33 Which of these is the lowest part of the human brain stem?

    a. cerebrum

    b. islets of langerhans

    c. medulla oblongata

34 **TRUE OR FALSE?** If the Rh antigen is present in blood, the blood is positive.

35 DNA is the chemical that controls how cells behave and reproduce. What word does the letter "A" stand for in "DNA"?

36 Which of the following are typically the strongest muscles in the human body?

    a. biceps femoris

    b. gluteus maximus

    c. triceps

37 Also called the windpipe, what tube in the human body carries air to and from the lungs?

38 The typical human heart has how many atria?

39 Otherwise known as folic acid, which B vitamin can be found in asparagus, broccoli, and liver?

40 What is the name of the muscle that pushes and pulls air into the lungs?

41 Melatonin is a hormone in the human body that helps regulate our sleep cycles. What is the name of the endocrine gland that produces melatonin?

42 Along with the cornea, what membrane, whose name comes from the Greek for "hard," forms the external covering of the human eyeball?

43 In general, human DNA contains how many pairs of chromosomes?

44 First discovered in 1921, what hormone secreted by the pancreas regulates how the body uses sugar?

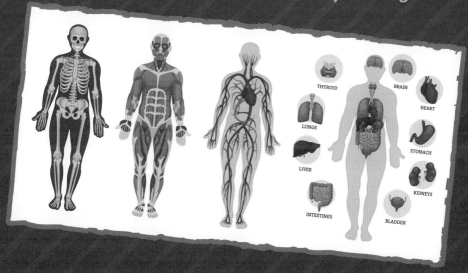

THYROID
BRAIN
HEART
LUNGS
STOMACH
LIVER
KIDNEYS
INTESTINES
BLADDER

BONUS WHAT PART OF THE HUMAN BRAIN UNDERNEATH THE CEREBRUM HELPS REGULATE BODY TEMPERATURE, SLEEP, AND APPETITE?

INSIDE THE
BODY

1 WHICH OF THE FOLLOWING ORGANS IN THE HUMAN BODY IS USED FOR THINKING?

A. KIDNEY   B. HEART
C. BRAIN

2 WHICH OF THE FOLLOWING ORGANS IS PRIMARILY RESPONSIBLE FOR MAINTAINING YOUR BALANCE?

A. EARS   B. EYES   C. NOSE

3 BY DEFINITION, THE WORD "NASAL" REFERS TO WHAT ORGAN IN THE HUMAN BODY?

4 CORONARY ARTERIES ARE VESSELS THAT BRING BLOOD TO WHAT ORGAN?

5 WHICH OF THE FOLLOWING PARTS OF THE EYE IS CLOSEST TO THE OPTIC NERVE?

A. IRIS   B. RETINA   C. CORNEA

6 IN THE HUMAN BODY, THORACIC NERVES ARE LOCATED IN THE THORAX, WHICH CONTAINS WHICH OF THE FOLLOWING ORGANS?

A. SMALL AND LARGE INTESTINE   B. HEART AND LUNGS

C. CEREBELLUM AND TEMPORAL LOBE

7 THE HAMMER BONE IS LOCATED IN WHICH OF THE FOLLOWING ORGANS IN THE HUMAN BODY?

A. EAR   B. NOSE   C. KIDNEY

8 THE CORNEA IS A PART OF WHICH ORGAN IN THE HUMAN BODY?

9 IF MR. CENA HAS A CLOG IN HIS EUSTACHIAN TUBE, HE HAS A CLOG IN WHICH ORGAN?

A. EAR   B. LUNGS   C. SMALL INTESTINE

10 WHAT ORGAN IN THE HUMAN BODY REMOVES WASTE FROM THE BLOOD AND DESTROYS OLD RED BLOOD CELLS?

11 WHAT ORGAN IN THE HUMAN BODY CONTAINS THE LENS?

12 THE VENA CAVA IS A VEIN ATTACHED TO THE RIGHT ATRIUM OF WHAT ORGAN IN THE HUMAN BODY?

13 THE COCHLEA, WHICH IS A SPIRAL TUBE CONTAINING NERVE ENDINGS, IS PART OF WHAT ORGAN?

14 LOCATED IN THE LUNGS, ALVEOLI ARE SMALL AIR SACS WHOSE PRIMARY ROLE IS TO ALLOW THE BLOOD TO EXCHANGE OXYGEN FOR WHAT OTHER GAS?

15 FROM THE GREEK WORD FOR "SIDE," WHAT IS THE SCIENTIFIC NAME FOR THE MEMBRANE THAT COVERS THE HUMAN LUNG?

16 THE CEREBELLUM IS PART OF WHAT ORGAN IN THE HUMAN BODY?

17 WHAT ORGAN IN THE HUMAN BODY HAS PLEURAL FLUID?

18 GALLBLADDER OR APPENDIX: IN THE HUMAN BODY, WHICH ORGAN IS USED TO STORE BILE?

19 WHAT ORGAN OF THE HUMAN BODY CONTAINS TINY FILTERS CALLED NEPHRONS, WHICH SEPARATE WASTE FROM USEFUL MATERIAL IN THE BLOOD?

BONUS THE DUODENUM IS PART OF WHICH ORGAN OF THE HUMAN BODY?

ANSWER KEY

AMAZING ANIMALS!

"A" IS FOR ANIMALS

1. a
2. a
3. a
4. a
5. c
6. a
7. a
8. b
9. a
10. a
11. c
12. b
13. c
14. (African) elephant
15. Australia
16. moose
17. amphibian
18. kangaroo
19. silk
20. polar (bear) (also accept: ursus maritimus, white bear, sea bear, ice bear)
21. giraffe
22. tiger
23. Africa
24. Australia

25. (American) buffalo (also accept: American bison)
26. Africa
27. dermis
28. horse
29. cod
Bonus: fox
30. true
31. true
32. true
33. true
34. false
35. false
36. true
37. false
38. false
39. false
40. true
41. false
42. true
43. true
44. true
45. true
46. true
47. true
48. false
49. true
50. true
51. true
52. true
53. true
54. false

EVERYTHING REPTILES

1. true
2. false
3. true
4. (sea) turtle
5. true
6. false
7. true
8. komodo dragon
9. a
10. Gila monster

DEEP IN THE OCEAN

1. false
2. b
3. false
4. c
5. true
6. true
7. c
8. true
9. false
10. a
11. shark
12. true
13. true
14. killer whale (also accept: orca, orca whales)
15. a
16. c
17. c

18. echinoderms (also accept: Echinodermata)
19. cephalopod (also accept: Cephalopoda)
Bonus: blue whale

BIRD WATCHING

1. 2
2. true
3. 5
4. goose
5. 1
6. true
7. true
8. ostrich
9. false
10. c
11. a
12. eagle

ALL ABOUT BUGS

1. true
2. c
3. female
4. butterfly
Bonus: chrysalis (or pupa)
5. true
6. 6
7. b
8. true
9. b
10. false
11. true
12. false
13. head
14. true
15. c
16. 10,000

CATS & DOGS

1. false
2. c
3. 2
4. false
5. cat (also accept: house cat)
6. 24
7. Mexico
8. 3
9. Dogs

DIGGING DINOSAURS

1. true
2. b
3. b
4. false
5. b
6. 2
7. c
8. false
9. Jurassic
10. a

SUPER SPACE

TO THE MOON AND BACK

1. United States
2. sun
3. true
4. lunar
5. Neptune
6. Mars
7. true
8. Titan
9. Uranus
10. Neptune

Bonus: Ganymede

SEEING STARS

1. 1
2. a
3. Polaris (North Star)
4. b
5. Taurus
6. Ursa Minor (do not accept: Ursa Major, Big Dipper)
7. Pegasus
8. Draco
9. Sirius (also accept: the Dog Star)

THE PLANETS

1. Earth
2. true
3. Jupiter
4. true
5. Jupiter
6. Mercury
7. Venus
8. Jupiter
9. Jupiter
10. Venus
11. 4
12. Mars
13. 4
14. b
15. 4
16. Uranus
17. b
18. true
19. Uranus
20. Earth
21. Venus

SPACE EXPLORATION

1. space

2. Earth
3. Mars
4. Russia (also accept: USSR)
5. Skylab (1)
6. Ed White
7. Gemini
Bonus: Apollo 8
8. dog
9. Edwin "Buzz" Aldrin
10. 1972
Bonus: Alan Shepard
11. Sputnik
Bonus: Luna 2
12. Mercury

EARTH ROCKS

1. c
2. moon
3. a
4. true
5. b
6. b
7. mesosphere
8. oxygen
Bonus: asthenosphere
Bonus: 8 minutes

THE SOLAR SYSTEM

1. false
2. the Milky Way
3. a
4. moon
5. false
6. two
7. the sun
8. false
9. b
10. a
11. Pluto

12. a
13. c
14. Mars
15. the sun
16. solar system, Milky Way galaxy, universe
17. hydrogen
18. c
19. 2
20. Andromeda
21. nebula
Bonus: the 2060s

EXPLORE THE USA

US PRESIDENTS

1. Thomas Jefferson
2. a
3. Virginia
4. 2
Bonus: Woodrow Wilson
5. a
6. Republican (also accept: GOP)
7. John F. Kennedy
8. Virginia
9. George Washington
10. a
Bonus: Hannibal Hamlin
11. Thomas Jefferson
12. Chester Arthur
13. Abraham Lincoln
14. Franklin Roosevelt
15. James Madison
16. Warren Harding
Bonus: John Tyler
17. Thomas Jefferson

18. Zachary Taylor
19. John F. Kennedy
20. Dwight D. Eisenhower
21. Franklin D. Roosevelt
22. Chester
23. Dwight D. Eisenhower
24. false
25. Thomas Jefferson
Bonus: Millard Fillmore
26. James Buchanan
27. Theodore Roosevelt
28. Richard Nixon
29. Abigail Adams
30. Harry Truman
31. Woodrow Wilson
32. 1799
33. 35
34. John C. Calhoun
35. Theodore Roosevelt
36. Dwight D. Eisenhower
Bonus: Dwight D. Eisenhower

THE FIFTY STATES

1. Pacific
2. Delaware
3. New York City
4. false
5. Ohio
6. true
7. Alaska
8. Denver
9. a
10. Florida
11. Washington
Bonus: 11

12. Everglades
    National Park
13. Library of
    Congress
14. Illinois
15. Bismarck
16. Q
Bonus: Colorado
17. Tennessee
18. California
Bonus: Utah
19. Staten Island
20. Tennessee
21. 6
22. Montana
23. Arkansas,
    Louisiana, New
    Mexico, Oklahoma
24. Tennessee and
    North Carolina
25. North Dakota
26. b
27. Missouri
28. Lake Ontario
29. Alaska
30. Maine
31. 8
32. Santa Fe (New
    Mexico)
33. Washington
Bonus: Santa Fe (New
    Mexico)

HISTORY

1. Pennsylvania
   Avenue
2. true
3. "liberty and justice
   for all"
4. Lincoln Memorial
5. Washington, DC
6. Vermont
7. 1876
8. (Dolley) Madison
9. false

10. b
11. Iowa
12. Hawaii
13. truths
14. Lincoln Memorial
15. 3
16. Monticello
17. true
Bonus: Battle of
    Bunker Hill
18. Spain
19. c
20. California
21. Pearl Harbor
22. 19th (also accept:
    1800s)
23. c
24. a
25. April 18
26. a
27. the War of 1812
28. Tennessee
29. New York
30. Georgia
31. Squanto
    (also accept:
    Tisquantum)
32. Valley Forge,
    Pennsylvania
33. Massachusetts
34. 1803
35. 1865
Bonus: Rhode Island
36. Spain
37. Sacramento
Bonus: 11
38. Rhode Island
39. Utah
40. Louisiana
41. Philadelphia
42. Louisiana
43. Pennsylvania
44. Harry Truman
45. Kentucky
46. Jeannette Rankin

47. William Lloyd
    Garrison
48. Samuel Tilden
49. South Carolina
50. Brooklyn Bridge
51. Powhatan
    (also accept:
    Wahunsonacock)
Bonus: Colorado

US GOVERNMENT

1. Tuesday
2. true
3. b
4. 1
5. b
6. 1st Amendment
Bonus: 18th
    Amendment
7. (the US) Capitol
    (building)
8. false
9. true
10. 8th Amendment
11. Virginia
12. a
13. (US) Constitution
14. a
15. executive
16. 2
17. a
Bonus: *Marbury v.
    Madison*
18. c
19. a
20. true
21. b
22. air force
23. captain
24. judicial
25. vice president
26. false
27. c
Bonus: January 3

28. b
29. 3
30. 75 percent (also accept: ¾)
31. Stamp Act
32. 9th Amendment
33. Pennsylvania
34. Senate
35. 4th Amendment
36. 9
37. Thurgood Marshall
38. the Articles of Confederation
39. Massachusetts
40. Bureau of Land Management
41. attorney general
42. National Archives
43. 67
Bonus: 19th Amendment

ARTS & CULTURE

WORKS OF ART

1. b
2. 3 (also accept: all of them)
3. the Louvre
4. yellow
5. silhouette
6. Washington, DC
7. United States
8. Michelangelo
9. Vincent van Gogh
10. Italy
11. (John) Audubon
12. David
13. Mona Lisa
14. (the)

Netherlands (also accept: Holland)
15. Spain
16. St. Petersburg

BOOKS, BOOKS, BOOKS

1. Christopher Robin
2. Pea
3. b
4. a
5. Wilbur
6. Aesop
7. 60
8. grapes
9. *The Wind in the Willows*
10. Alexandre Dumas
11. Mark Twain (also accept: Samuel Clemens)
12. Sherlock Holmes
13. "Rip Van Winkle"
14. Benjamin Franklin
15. United States
16. Ebenezer
17. *The Prince and the Pauper*
18. Jane Austen
19. *Othello*
20. *Old Yeller*
21. Jack London (also accept: John London, John Chaney)
22. *Hamlet*
23. Little House (also Little House on the Prairie)
24. *Charlotte's Web*
25. a
Bonus: Edgar Allan Poe
26. protagonist

27. Charles Dickens
28. the Montagues
29. Robert Louis Stevenson
30. Robert Frost
31. Helen of Troy
32. Charles Dickens
33. *To Kill a Mockingbird*
34. *The Secret Garden*
35. James Fenimore Cooper
36. *Gulliver's Travels*
37. Geoffrey Chaucer
38. Emily Dickinson
39. 10
40. 14
41. Jules Verne
42. *The Hobbit*
43. Mary Shelley
44. Charlotte Brontë
45. *A Tale of Two Cities*
46. *The Scarlet Letter*
47. Rudyard Kipling
48. Julius Caesar
49. *The Swiss Family Robinson*
50. Dr. (John) Watson
51. Dante
52. Potter
Bonus: William Golding
53. Langston Hughes
54. *The Great Gatsby*
55. *A Connecticut Yankee in King Arthur's Court* (also accept: *A Yankee at the Court of King Arthur*)
56. Hans Christian Andersen

MUSIC CLASS

1. b
2. 6
3. 4
4. 5
5. b
6. 3
7. 3
8. a
9. Tennessee
10. Russia (do not accept: USSR; Soviet Union)
11. forte
12. 4
13. Sleeping Beauty
14. 7
15. Woody Guthrie
16. *William Tell*

LET'S MAKE MUSIC

1. true
2. brass
3. a
4. a
5. triangle
6. false
7. a
8. Scotland
9. b
10. true
11. b
12. a
13. drum
14. c
15. a
16. piccolo
17. tuba
18. false
19. c
20. oboe
21. violin
22. woodwind

THE MUSIC SHOW

1. Italy
2. Wolfgang Amadeus Mozart
3. a
4. John Philip Sousa
5. Igor Stravinsky
6. Ira (also accept: Israel)
7. (Wolfgang Amadeus) Mozart
8. 9
9. Johann Sebastian
10. *The Nutcracker*
11. (Johann Sebastian) Bach

BACK TO SCHOOL

GRAMMAR & ENGLISH

1. a
2. false
3. two
4. verb
5. b
6. enormous
7. b
8. b
9. b
10. b
11. c
12. kayak
13. b
14. b
15. a
16. two
17. a
18. c
19. false
20. c
21. c
22. 2
23. 1

MATH SKILLS

1. x
2. 79
3. 21
4. 5
5. 6
6. 1
7. 627
8. ⅛
9. false
10. 15
11. b
12. true
13. 7
14. 84
15. ⁹/₁₂ (also accept: ¾ or 75%)
16. 90 (degrees)
17. three
18. 12
19. 64
20. 36
21. 0.34
22. 40%
23. pi
24. 10
25. 64
26. a
27. 1
28. 70
29. 12.4
30. 3
31. 1
32. 10,000 (ten thousand)
33. 200
34. negative 12
35. 10

CURIOUS ABOUT SCIENCE

1. c
2. b
3. true
4. b
5. true
6. igneous
7. false
8. false
9. true
10. braille
11. true
12. a
13. true
14. true
Bonus: Kelvin scale
15. blue
16. violet
17. c
18. ultraviolet
19. true
20. c
Bonus: limestone
21. b
22. a
23. three
24. penicillin
Bonus: ion
25. a
Bonus: protium
26. current
27. a
28. pounds per square inch
29. galvanometer (also accept: rheoscope)
Bonus: 10
30. proton
31. 14
32. fungus (also accept: fungi)
33. true
34. hydrogen
35. 6
36. joule
37. hazardous materials
38. neutron(s)
39. acceleration
40. inertia
41. cilia (also accept: cilium, plural)
42. nitrogen

LEARNING SHAPES

1. c
2. b
3. 12
4. 30 inches
5. 4
6. 100 feet
7. 4
8. 2
9. 6
10. a
11. c
12. b
13. 2
14. b
15. false
16. 7
17. 7
18. 8
19. true
20. 8
21. 9
22. 1
23. 2
24. circle
25. 0
26. 178
27. 1080
28. 3
29. 11
30. 7
Bonus: 6 inches

THE ELEMENTS

1. a
2. c
3. true
4. oxygen
5. sulfur
6. helium
7. iron
Bonus: Pb
8. chlorine
9. platinum
10. hydrogen
11. oxygen
12. carbon dioxide (CO_2)
13. lithium
14. helium
15. uranium
Bonus: zirconium

ALL AROUND US

MEASURING FUN!

1. 24
2. true
3. a
4. false
5. 63
6. b
7. 117 ounces
8. a
9. 60
10. 2
11. 1440
12. mile
13. 24
14. 10 quarts
15. 1 billon
16. (Anders) Celsius
17. 3

MONEY MATH

1. false
2. dime
3. false
4. b
5. 8 dollars
6. $3.74
7. $186.41
8. $10 bill
9. nickels
10. Thomas Jefferson
11. (Danish) krone (also accept: crown)
Bonus: Poland

DAYS, WEEKS, AND MONTHS

1. Thanksgiving
2. 36
3. 31
4. false
5. 31
6. False
7. November 25
Bonus: June
8. summer and fall (also accept: summer and autumn)
9. Monday
10. May 1
11. Christopher Columbus
12. December 30
13. 14
14. March
15. November
16. 168

TALK ABOUT TIME!

1. 11:00 a.m.
2. 7
3. 53
4. 5 hours and 15 minutes (also accept: 315 minutes)
5. 12:00 p.m. (also accept: noon, twelve o'clock)
6. 150

LET'S TALK SPORTS

1. Amira
2. ball
3. 8
4. 160
5. 7
6. basketball
7. a
8. 10

CARS, TRAINS, SHIPS, AND PLANES

1. c
2. a
3. b
4. NASA (also accept: National Aeronautics and Space Administration)
5. Pony Express
6. (Henry) Ford
7. zeppelin (do not accept: blimp)
8. 1957

9. 6 hours and 40 minutes (also accept: 400 minutes, 6 ⅔ hours)
10. b
11. 1,820 miles
12. 10,560 ft.

FOOD & DRINK

1. 3
2. 11
3. c
4. true
5. 35
6. 24
7. 6

THE GREAT OUTDOORS

EXPLORE THE OCEAN

1. Pacific Ocean
2. Indian Ocean
3. true
4. Pacific Ocean
5. Atlantic
6. Arctic
7. Indian Ocean
8. Atlantic
9. b
10. 4
11. Indian Ocean

WILD WEATHER

1. false
2. true
3. true
4. a

5. a
6. a
7. true
8. a
Bonus: The Coriolis
effect

MOUNTAINS OF THE WORLD

1. Asia
2. b
3. North America
4. Colorado
5. Greece
6. b
7. South America
8. Himalayas
9. Washington
10. the Andes
11. Russia
12. Antarctica
13. Arkansas
14. Japan
15. a
16. India
17. Missouri
18. Germany
19. Mont Blanc
20. Cascade Range
21. Mount
    Kilimanjaro

RAGING RIVERS

1. Nile River
2. Mississippi River
3. Louisiana
4. Mexico
5. false
6. Indiana
7. b
8. Missouri River
9. Delaware River
10. Minnesota

11. (Republic of)
    Ireland (do not
    accept: Northern
    Ireland)
12. Delaware River
13. Potomac
14. Australia
15. Idaho
16. Yangtze
17. Danube
18. Victoria Falls
19. Anacostia River
20. (Bay of) Bengal
21. St. Lawrence River
22. Mackenzie River
23. Savannah River
24. Henry
25. Alaska

ERUPTING VOLCANOES!

1. true
2. true
3. a
4. Mauna Kea
5. the Philippines
6. c
7. Mars
8. Mount Vesuvius
9. Sicily

LAKE WONDERS

1. false
2. Canada
3. a
4. California
5. Lake Superior
6. New York
7. Lake Ontario
8. Lake Erie
9. 4
10. 8
11. Hudson

Bonus: Lake Baikal

PARKS ROAD TRIP

1. Yellowstone
2. true
3. Yellowstone
   (National Park)
4. c
5. Maui
6. Nevada
7. c
8. California
9. Massachusetts
10. John Muir
Bonus: Arkansas
11. b
12. true
13. Kentucky

SEE THE SEAS

1. c
2. Asia
3. Greece
4. Caspian Sea
5. Italy
6. Red Sea
7. Black Sea
8. Europe
9. Mediterranean
   (Sea)
10. Aegean Sea
11. Sicily

PLANT LIFE

1. true
2. b
3. c
4. Arbor Day
Bonus: cambium
5. true
6. b

7. true
8. true
9. a
10. b
11. b
12. b
13. false
14. b
15. true
16. true
17. carbon dioxide
(also accept CO_2)
18. c
19. legumes
20. b
21. (bristlecone) pine
22. green
23. vitamin E

PEOPLE & PLACES

AROUND THE GLOBE

1. Spain
2. Asia
3. 2
4. Canada
5. Europe
6. Mexico
7. Egypt
8. Antarctica
9. Antarctica
10. Asia
11. Iceland
Bonus: Haiti
12. b
13. Japan
14. east
15. c
Bonus: Mekong
16. c
17. c

18. true
19. Honshu
20. Ming (Dynasty)
21. Iceland
22. South America
23. a
24. South America
25. Malaysia
Bonus: Greenwich
26. Germany
27. a
28. Africa
29. Romania
30. Verrazzano
(Narrows Bridge)
31. (Great) Britain
(also accept:
England, the
U.K., the United
Kingdom)
32. St. Petersburg
(also accept:
Leningrad,
Petrograd)
33. Cuba
34. Quebec
35. Japan
Bonus: Canada
Bonus: Bay of Bengal
36. Paris
37. Ecuador
38. Ankara
39. Mexico
40. 1960s
41. Greece
42. the Philippines
Bonus: Tanzania
43. Russia
44. Africa
45. Argentina
Bonus: 1912
46. Spain
47. *Lusitania*

48. (Union of)
Myanmar (also
accept: Burma)
49. 31
50. Guam
51. Damascus
52. Switzerland
Bonus: Nepal
53. Portugal
54. Warsaw Pact
55. Caspian Sea
56. Wales
57. Byzantium
58. China
59. Corsica
Bonus: the
Lighthouse of
Alexandria

HISTORICAL FIGURES

1. Thomas Edison
2. Alexander Graham
Bell
Bonus: Igor Sikorsky
3. b
4. Morse (code)
5. Benjamin Franklin
6. Charles Lindbergh
Bonus: Matthew
Perry
7. Louis Pasteur
8. Air Force One
Bonus: the speed of
light
9. (Nikola) Tesla
10. the Duke of
Wellington (also
accept: Arthur
Wellesley)
Bonus: Sir Francis
Drake
11. Hernando Cortez

EXTRAORDINARY WOMEN

1. England (also accept: the U.K., United Kingdom, Great Britain, Britain)
2. Susan B. Anthony
3. 1981
4. physics
5. Florence Nightingale
6. Israel
7. Sojourner Truth
8. Victoria Woodhull
9. Anne Sullivan (Macy) (also accept: Annie Sullivan, Joanna Sullivan)
10. Rosa Parks (also: Rosa Louise McCauley)
11. the American Red Cross

INTO THE UNKNOWN

1. 1492
2. Pacific
3. 3
4. a
5. Ferdinand
Bonus: Bartolomeu Dias
Bonus: Francisco Pizarro
6. Pennsylvania
7. William Penn
8. Sir Henry Morton Stanley
9. Norway
10. a
11. China
12. Shoshone
13. Hernando de Soto (also accept: Fernando de Soto)
Bonus: (Francisco Vásquez de) Coronado
14. Samuel de Champlain
Bonus: Johannes Kepler
15. India
16. Detroit
Bonus: Palos (de la Frontera)

KINGS, QUEENS, AND RULERS

1. 3
2. Henry VII
3. Genghis Khan
4. Macedonia (also accept Macedon)
5. France
6. King Charles (II)
7. Maryland
8. (Queen) Guinevere (also accept: Guenever)
Bonus: Charles I
Bonus: King John
9. (King) George III
10. Hideki Tojo
11. Attila
12. Joseph Stalin
13. Cleopatra
Bonus: James Stuart (also accept: James, King James)
14. Ivan (the Great)
Bonus: Hammurabi
15. Emperor Hirohito (also accept: Emperor Shōwa)
16. Queen Elizabeth (also accept: Elizabeth I)
17. King Louis XVI
18. Charlemagne (Charles the Great)
Bonus: King Philip II (of Macedon)

ANCIENT HISTORY

1. the moon
2. a
3. b
4. (Ancient) Egyptians (also accept: Egypt, Ancient Egypt)
5. (Ancient) Egypt (also accept: Egyptians)
6. c
7. 29
8. a
9. (Julius) Caesar (also accept: Gaius Julius Caesar; do not accept: Caesar Augustus)
10. fire
11. Asia
12. Babylon
13. a
14. b
15. Nero (also accept: Lucius)
16. Cupid
17. (Ancient) Greek
18. Athena
19. Aphrodite
20. Bacchus

21. Crete
22. Turkey
23. Hannibal
24. Euphrates
25. Julius Caesar
26. Pericles
27. New Zealand
28. (the) Colossus of
    Rhodes
Bonus: Africa

EVERYTHING MYTHOLOGY

1. Earth
2. true
3. Atlas
4. Zeus (do not
   accept: Jupiter)
5. Pandora
6. faun(s)
7. Pan
8. Hercules
9. a
10. Hydra
11. Olympic torch
    (flame)
12. Perseus
13. Neptune
14. Diana
15. Ares
16. Hades
17. Narcissus
18. Apollo

EXPLORE THE HUMAN BODY

THE FANTASTIC BODY

1. 2
2. true
3. true
4. cavity

5. true
6. true
7. b
8. c
9. c
10. a
11. b
12. true
13. true
14. Libia
15. larynx
16. true
17. b
18. false
19. c
20. b
21. resuscitation
22. b
23. a
24. false
25. b
26. knee (also accept:
    patella)
27. b
28. a
29. 12
30. bicep
31. b
32. thyroid
33. c
34. true
35. acid
36. b
37. trachea
38. two
39. vitamin B9
40. the diaphragm
41. pineal gland
42. sclera
43. 23
44. insulin
Bonus: hypothalamus

INSIDE THE BODY

1. c
2. a
3. nose
4. heart
5. b
6. b
7. a
8. eye
9. a
10. liver
11. eye
12. heart
13. ear
14. carbon dioxide
15. pleura (also
    accept: pleurae,
    visceral pleura,
    parietal pleura)
16. brain
17. lungs
18. gallbladder
19. kidney
Bonus: small
    intestine

COVER

1.a
2.Uranus

PHOTO CREDITS

COVER

(rhinoceros) EcoPic/iStock/Getty Images Plus, (Uranus) forplayday/iStock/Getty Images Plus

TABLE OF CONTENTS

2–3: (chalkboard and school supplies) eternalcreative/iStock/Getty Images Plus

INTRODUCTION

4–5: (chalkboard) Smilja Jovanovic/iStock/Getty Images Plus

MEET THE CLASSMATES

6–7: (chalkboard) Smilja Jovanovic/iStock/Getty Images Plus

AMAZING ANIMALS!

8–9: (tree frogs) Jrleyland/iStock/Getty Images Plus; 10: (fawn) JNevitt/iStock/Getty Images Plus; 11: (marmot) MirasWonderland/iStock/Getty Images Plus; 12: (polar bear) Alexey_Seafarer/iStock/Getty Images Plus; 13: (lemurs) Enjoylife2/iStock/Getty Images Plus; 14: (owl) WhitcombeRD/iStock/Getty Images Plus; 15: (duck) DmitriMaruta/iStock/Getty Images Plus, (giraffe) Rich Townsend/iStock/Getty Images Plus; 16–17: (crocodile) Joe Pearl Photography/iStock/Getty Images Plus; 18: (sea urchin) Eduardo Baena/iStock/Getty Images Plus; 19: (humpback whale) PaulWolf/iStock/Getty Images Plus; 20–21: (penguin) fieldwork/iStock/Getty Images Plus; 21: (hummingbird) drferry/iStock/Getty Images Plus; 22: (butterfly) Amy Newton-McConnel/iStock/Getty Images Plus; 23: (bee) DanielPrudek/iStock/Getty Images Plus; 24: (kitten) Sonsedska/iStock/Getty Images Plus, (chihuahua) GlobalP/iStock/Getty Images Plus; 24–25: (cat and dog) Voren1/iStock/Getty Images Plus; 26: (pterodactyl) Warpaintcobra/iStock/Getty Images Plus, (Tyrannosaurus rex) digitalgenetics/iStock/Getty Images Plus; 27: (brachiosaurus) dottedhippo/iStock/Getty Images Plus

SUPER SPACE

28–29: (telescope and night sky) ClaudioVentrella/iStock/Getty Images Plus; 30: (moon) robertsrob/iStock/Getty Images Plus; 31: (Jupiter moons) alexaldo/iStock/Getty Images Plus; 32–33: (night sky) Allexxandar/iStock/Getty Images Plus; 34: (Earth) Thanapol sinsrang/iStock/Getty Images Plus; 35: (Saturn's rings) Digital Vision./iStock/Getty Images Plus; 36–37: (Jupiter) alexaldo/iStock/Getty Images Plus; 38: (astronaut) alex_skp/iStock/Getty Images Plus; 40–41: (view of Earth from space) studio023/iStock/Getty Images Plus; 41: (Earth inset) robertsrob/iStock/Getty Images Plus; 42: (galaxy) lakshmipathi lucky/iStock/Getty Images Plus; 43: (asteroids) dottedhippo/iStock/Getty Images Plus

EXPLORE THE USA

44–45: (flag) Maksym Kapliuk/iStock/Getty Images Plus; 46: (Lincoln Memorial) LionelHKR/iStock/Getty Images Plus; 47: (George Washington) Photos.com/iStock/Getty Images Plus; 48: (Mount Rushmore) scgerding/iStock/Getty Images Plus; 50: (water lilies) Wildnerdpix/iStock/Getty Images Plus; 51: (Statue of Liberty) spyarm/iStock/Getty Images Plus, (black sand beach) Tom Simak/iStock/Getty Images Plus; 52: (Zion National Park) Joecho-16/iStock/Getty Images Plus; 53: (Ruby Beach) lightphoto/iStock/Getty Images Plus; 54: (Liberty Bell) rabbit75_ist/iStock/Getty Images Plus; 55: (Valley Forge) DelmasLehman/iStock/Getty Images Plus; 56: (Constitution) oersin/iStock/Getty Images Plus; 57: (cannon) Bill Chizek/iStock/Getty Images Plus; 58: (Civil War soldiers) Georgethefourth/iStock/Getty Images Plus; 59: (White House) tupungato/iStock/Getty Images Plus; 60: (gavel) neirfy/iStock/Getty Images Plus; 61: (Supreme Court building) sframephoto/iStock/Getty Images Plus; 62: (soldiers) MivPiv/iStock/Getty Images Plus; 63: (George Washington) TonyBaggett/iStock/Getty Images Plus; 64: (Benjamin Franklin) WaffOzzy/iStock/Getty Images Plus; 65: (Capitol building) dkfielding/iStock/Getty Images Plus

ARTS & CULTURE

66–67: (guitar) ipopba/iStock/Getty Images Plus; 68: (painting) Jupiterimages/iStock/Getty Images Plus, (Lourve) MasterLu/iStock/Getty Images Plus; 69: (painting) Jupiterimages/iStock/Getty Images Plus; 70: (books) artisteer/iStock/Getty Images Plus, (Brothers Grimm) Photos.com/iStock/Getty Images Plus; 72: (Jane Austen) GeorgiosArt/iStock/Getty Images Plus; 74: (book and rose) eurobanks/iStock/Getty Images Plus; 75: (Charles Dickens) FPG/iStock/Getty Images Plus; 76: (ballet shoes) Kuzmichstudio/iStock/Getty Images Plus; 77: (DJ background) Ivan_Neru/iStock/Getty Images Plus, (musical notes) chaluk/iStock/Getty Images Plus; 78–79: (trumpet) Furtseff/iStock/Getty Images Plus; 80–81: (bagpipes) Lukassek/iStock/Getty Images Plus; 82: (sheet music) luvemakphoto/iStock/Getty Images Plus; 83: (Johann Sebastian Bach) jopelka/iStock/Getty Images Plus

BACK TO SCHOOL

84–85: (chalkboard and school supplies) virojt/iStock/Getty Images Plus; 86: (mouse) CreativeNature_nl/iStock/Getty Images Plus; 88: (piggy bank) marchmeena29/iStock/Getty Images Plus; 89: (quoits) eyepark/iStock/Getty Images Plus; 91: (pizza) Mizina/iStock/Getty Images Plus; 92: (atom particles) vchal/iStock/Getty Images Plus; 93: (visual sound waves) HARR120N/iStock/Getty Images Plus; 94: (chemistry set) Daviziro/iStock/Getty Images Plus; 95: (high-speed connection) Thomas-Soellner/iStock/Getty Images Plus; 96: (virtual molecular structure) everythingpossible/iStock/Getty Images Plus; 97: (chemical elements) ktsimage/iStock/Getty Images Plus; 98: (rainbow toy blocks) 3d_kot/iStock/Getty Images Plus, (dice) LanternWorks/iStock/Getty Images Plus; 99: (race track) efks/iStock/Getty Images Plus; 100: (stop sign) ronniechua/iStock/Getty Images Plus; 101: (blackboard) Bigmouse108/iStock/Getty Images Plus; 102–103: (periodic table of elements) lucadp/iStock/Getty Images Plus

ALL AROUND US

104–105: (running with balloons) Vasyl Dolmatov/iStock/Getty Images Plus; 106: (toothpicks) dinna79/iStock/Getty Images Plus; 107: (ice-cream cones) VeselovaElena/iStock/Getty Images Plus; 108–109: (penny jar) John_Brueske/iStock/Getty Images Plus; 109: (penny inset) peterspiro/iStock/Getty Images Plus; 110: (fall table) ChristinaFelsing/iStock/Getty Images Plus, (calendar) Tatomm/iStock/Getty Images Plus; 111: (tulip garden) Supersmario/iStock/Getty Images Plus; 112–113: (clock) anyaberkut/iStock/Getty Images Plus; 114: (baseball) manusapon kasosod/iStock/Getty Images Plus; 115: (football) dehooks/iStock/Getty Images Plus, (archery) Jovana Kuzmanovic/iStock/Getty Images Plus; 116: (submarine) ambassador806/iStock/Getty Images Plus, (airplane) aapsky/iStock/Getty Images Plus; 117: (train) scanrail/iStock/Getty Images Plus; 118–119: (lemonade) jenifoto/iStock/Getty Images Plus

THE GREAT OUTDOORS

120–121: (lake sunrise) Paul Hartley/iStock/Getty Images Plus; 122–123: (tropical sea) IakovKalinin/iStock/Getty Images Plus; 124: (clouds) Christian Horz/iStock/Getty Images Plus, (tulip field) TomasSereda/iStock/Getty Images Plus; 125: (tornado) Meindert van der Haven/iStock/Getty Images Plus; 126: (Mount Sopris, top) haveseen/iStock/Getty Images Plus, (Ama Dablam, bottom) DanielPrudek/iStock/Getty Images Plus; 127: (national park in Kenya) Byrdyak/iStock/Getty Images Plus; 128: (Rybinsk) bbsferrari/iStock/Getty Images Plus; 129: (Mississippi River) Willard/iStock/Getty Images Plus; 130: (Miles Canyon) HeatherECampbell/iStock/Getty Images Plus; 131: (Schuylkill River) zullos/iStock/Getty Images Plus; 132–133: (volcanic eruption) Beboy_ltd/iStock/Getty Images Plus; 134: (Lake Superior) Jordan Schopper/iStock/Getty Images Plus; 135: (frozen bubbles) Streluk/iStock/Getty Images Plus; 136: (Muir Woods) ShaheenK/iStock/Getty Images Plus, (Old Faithful) Andrei Stanescu/iStock/Getty Images Plus; 137: (Makahiku Falls) estivillml/iStock/Getty Images Plus; 138–139: (yacht on the sea) Biletskiy_Evgeniy/iStock/Getty Images Plus; 139: (Amalfi) Aleh Varanishcha/iStock/Getty Images Plus; 140: (bamboo grove) blew_i/iStock/Getty Images Plus

PEOPLE & PLACES

142–143: (view of Istanbul) Carmian/iStock/Getty Images Plus; 144: (Wat Arun Temple) saiko3p/iStock/Getty Images Plus; 145: (overhead view of Bolivia) StreetFlash/iStock/Getty Images Plus; 146: (Victoria Harbour) NithidPhoto/iStock/Getty Images Plus, (Yosemite National Park) Eagle2308/iStock/Getty Images Plus; 147: (village in Greenland) Olga_Gavrilova/iStock/Getty Images Plus; 148: (ocean liner) MR1805/iStock/Getty Images Plus, (view from the Thames) Daniel Lange/iStock/Getty Images Plus; 149: (view of Reykjavik) potpongs/iStock/Getty Images Plus; 150: (Alexander Graham Bell) Photos.com/iStock/Getty Images Plus; 151: (the Golden Hind) CoreyFord/iStock/Getty Images Plus, (painting of Battle of Waterloo) Photos.com/iStock/Getty Images Plus; 152–153: (women working on WWII aircraft) George Marks/iStock/Getty Images Plus; 153: (Clara Barton) Photos.com/iStock/Getty Images Plus; 154: (children on safari) warrengoldswain/iStock/Getty Images Plus, (Skipanon River) WestWindGraphics/iStock/Getty Images Plus; 155: (Machu Picchu) sorincolac/iStock/Getty Images Plus; 156: (house on the Thousand Islands) demerzel21/iStock/Getty Images Plus; 157: (highway) Image Source/iStock/Getty Images Plus; 158: (Alexander the Great statue) paulshark/iStock/Getty Images Plus, (crown) tomertu/iStock/Getty Images Plus; 159: (sword in the stone) UroshPetrovic/iStock/Getty Images Plus, (Henrietta Maria of France) GeorgiosArt/iStock/Getty Images Plus; 160: (The Great Wall of China) aphotostory/iStock/Getty Images Plus; 161: (Elizabeth I) Photos.com/iStock/Getty Images Plus; 162: (ancient coins) kvkirillov/iStock/Getty Images Plus, (Roman villa) tingra/iStock/Getty Images Plus; 163: (mask) JoseIgnacioSoto/iStock/Getty Images Plus; 164: (Greek temple) Zarnell/iStock/Getty Images Plus; 165: (ancient relief) Gilmanshin/iStock/Getty Images Plus; 166: (ancient Greek pottery) Matriyoshka/iStock/Getty Images Plus; 167: (Aphrodite icon) MchlSkhrv/iStock/Getty Images Plus

EXPLORE THE HUMAN BODY

168–169: (neurons) whitehoune/iStock/Getty Images Plus; 170: (human circulatory system) magicmine/iStock/Getty Images Plus; 171: (hand X-ray) herraez/iStock/Getty Images Plus; 172: (body scan) Jackie Niam/iStock/Getty Images Plus; 173: (red blood cells) Thinkhubstudio/iStock/Getty Images Plus; 174: (brain activity) iLexx/iStock/Getty Images Plus; 175: (body structure) ikryannikovgmailcom/iStock/Getty Images Plus; 176–177: (DNA molecules) Design Cells/iStock/Getty Images Plus

ANSWER KEY, PHOTO CREDITS, COPYRIGHT

178–192: (chalkboard) Smilja Jovanovic/iStock/Getty Images Plus